Peter Goodgame

Peter Goodgame

The Globalists
& the Islamists:
Fomenting the
"Clash of Civilizations"
for a New World Order

OMNIA VERITAS

Peter Goodgame

Published by Omnia Veritas Ltd

$\mathcal{O}$MNIA VERITAS

contact@omniaveritas.org

www.omniaveritas.org

Table of Contents

The British, the Middle East and Radical Islam

I. Introduction

As the American government, led by the Bush Administration, fights its so-called "War on Terror" with plans to invade and overthrow Iraq, America's steadfast ally in this endeavor continues to be the British government of Tony Blair. The following study will take a look at the history of the region that America has become entangled in, a region that used to be, and to some degree still is, almost entirely controlled by Britain. Is this current "War on Terror" truly a war to bring freedom to the region and to promote traditional American ideals, or is it a power-play to solidify global American hegemony? And what does Britain have to gain?

Britain appears to be our greatest ally but it must be understood that British geo-strategists are the masters of political manipulation and subversion. Even as the physical British colonial empire was declining in the first half of this century they were already building the framework for a completely global empire based on the legacy of Cecil Rhodes utilizing the resources of the super-capitalists and financiers of New York and London. These elites may be predominantly British and American in nationality, but they reject democracy and the American Constitution and work against the best interests of British, American and international citizens. By studying the history of the Middle East, and the elitist manipulation of it, we can perhaps predict what is to come after this last final push of the American Empire. (Written in the fall of 2002)

II. Britain takes the Middle East

As documented in F. William Engdahl's book *A Century of War - Anglo-American Oil Politics and the New World Order,* Britain's interest in the Middle East was piqued when her leaders realized that oil would replace coal as the energy source of the future. At the turn of the century Britain had no first-hand access to oil and was dependent upon America, Russia or Mexico for her supplies. This was quickly understood as an unacceptable situation and through intrigues involving British spy Sidney Reilly and Australian geologist and engineer William Knox d'Arcy Britain was able to secure drilling rights to Persian oil from Persian monarch Reza Khan. D'Arcy paid what amounted to $20,000 cash for rights to tap Persian oil until 1961, with a 16% royalty from all sales going to the Shah. The British company that Reilly persuaded d'Arcy to ally with then became known as the Anglo-Persian Oil Company, which was a forerunner of the mighty British Petroleum (BP).

However, even with a supply of Persian oil, Britain was losing the race to secure Middle Eastern oil reserves to the Germans. In the years prior to World War I Germany had enjoyed an astonishing economic explosion and this was helped by her alliance with the Ottoman Empire which allowed her access to their vast reserves. In 1889 the Germans worked out an agreement to finance, through Deutsche Bank, a railway from Constantinople into Anatolia, and later in 1899 the final agreement for a complete Berlin-to-Baghdad railway was signed.

The British made sure that this rail link was never completed through the use of her ally Serbia, which stood in the middle of the German alliance that included Austro-Hungary, Bulgaria and the Ottoman Empire. World War I is commonly understood as sparked by the assassination of the Austrian Archduke Ferdinand by Serbian assassins. Serbia did play a key part in World War I, but the conflict was not simply a result of this solitary event. The truth is that World War I was fomented by the British so that they could control oil, foreseen by their geo-strategists as the world's most important emerging resource.[1]

In 1916, at the height of World War I, the British worked out an agreement with France, Italy and Russia known as the Sykes-Picot Agreement that carved up the Ottoman Empire into Western colonies. This secret agreement created the arbitrary boundaries of what are today the countries of Jordan, Syria, Lebanon, Iraq and Kuwait. Britain would control the oil-rich Persian Gulf through Iraq and Kuwait and would also receive Palestine and Jordan. France would receive Syria and Lebanon, Italy was promised parts of Anatolia and some Mediterranean islands and Russia was to get parts of Armenia and Kurdistan.

During the war Britain diverted more than 1.4 million troops from the Western Front to fight the Ottomans in the east. While the French lost 1.5 million dead and suffered 2.6 million wounded in the trenches the British gained victory after victory in the Middle East. After the

[1] *A Century of War - Anglo-American Oil Politics and the New World Order*, F. William Engdahl, 1993 pp. 30-36

war ended the British continued to maintain over a million troops in the area, and in 1918 the British General Allenby found that he was the de-facto military dictator over almost the entire Arab Middle East.[2]

While T.E. Lawrence was directing the Arab revolt against the Ottomans on behalf of the British he had assured his Arab allies that Britain would honor their desires for independence, but after the war these promises were ignored. During the war the famous Balfour Declaration was also given. It was a letter between Lord Balfour and Lord Rothschild that promised official British endorsement of a Jewish state in Palestine. The plain fact is that the Arabs were cheated, betrayed and used in a British drive to gain control of the region that contained the world's largest known oil reserves.

In the fight against the Ottoman Empire the British gained the support of two important Arab leaders. The first was Hussein I of the Hashemite dynasty, a dynasty that traced a direct lineage back to the prophet Mohammed. He was the ruler of the Hijaz area that included Mecca and Medina and the British hyped his "holy" status to maximize his popular support. The second prominent Arab leader that the British eventually brought into the fold was Ibn Saud, the leader of the tribal Wahhabi sect of central Arabia. Ibn Saud used his British financing to enhance his position as a religious figure and to buy the support of the Bedouins.

---

[2] Ibid pp. 50-52

After the Ottomans were defeated and the Sykes-Picot and Balfour Agreements were revealed Hussein I realized the treachery that had defeated him and he abdicated his throne. His three sons Ali, Faisal and Abdallah then tried their luck at Arab rule.

Prince Ali took over the Hijaz but lost it in 1925 in his clash with the forces of the British- supported Ibn Saud. The Saudis have ruled Arabia ever since. The biggest mistake Britain made was losing interest in the Saudis and the Arabian deserts, allowing Standard Oil of California to come in and purchase the rights to search for oil in Saudi Arabia for $250,000 in 1933.[3] Since that time the Saudi royal family has enjoyed a very special relationship with the United States.

Prince Faisal, who had worked with T.E. Lawrence and conquered Damascus from the Ottomans, made a claim to rule French-governed Syria in 1920, but the French ended this attempt after just four months. Faisal then retreated to Britain and a year later he was recycled when he, a Sunni prince, was given the predominantly Shia territory of Iraq to govern as king. Faisal I ruled until his death in 1933. His son Ghazi ruled Iraq until he died in 1939, followed by Ghazi's son Faisal II, the last king of Iraq, who was killed in a military coup in 1958.

The Hashemite dynasty continues to this day only through the third of our trio of Hussein's sons. Prince Abdallah was given the land of Trans-Jordan to govern

---

[3] *A Brutal Friendship - The West and the Arab Elite*, Said K. Aburish, 1997, p. 76

in 1921 and as king he maintained a strong pro-British stance, despite the treachery displayed to his father. Abdallah understood that there was no future in contradicting his masters, and the British used him to check the fury of his own population as the British desire to establish a Jewish state in Israel came into focus.

King Abdallah was killed in the Al Aqsa Mosque in 1951, and his sixteen year old grandson Hussein took the throne. King Hussein ruled until his death in 1999, and his son King Abdullah now rules the Hashemite Kingdom of Jordan.

The main point that must be understood from the historical record, as it relates to the main focus of this article, is the cynical manner in which the religion of Islam has been used by the British Empire to further British political goals. In the book by Arab historian Said Aburish, *A Brutal Friendship - The West and the Arab Elite,* the author identifies three distinct phases of Islam's relationship with the West within the 20th Century.[4]

The first phase, according to Aburish, was the phase immediately after World War I. The Arab leaders had been cheated and betrayed, but they were still dependent upon the British to allow them any type of rule over the Arab masses.

Ibn Saud was the leader of the Wahhabi sect, and the British acknowledged his influence as a religious figure

---

[4] Ibid p. 57

and funded his conquest of all of Arabia.

The Hashemites were the strongest traditional Arab force, but their back was broken when Ibn Saud threw them out of Mecca and Medina. In their "pity" the British then placed Abdallah and Faisal over Jordan and Iraq. These Hashemite princes were outsiders, to say the least, but the British played the religion card for all it was worth and justified their actions to the Arab people through the Hashemite lineage that traced back to Mohammed. Certainly any Arab would be happy to be ruled by a "holy" clan like the Hashemites!

The British used Islam in Palestine as well when, in 1921, they engineered the election of their choice, Haj Amin Husseini, a descendant of Mohammed, to the post of Grand Mufti of Jerusalem. In Palestine almost all of the elite Arab families quickly found it profitable to be pro- British, and the Grand Mufti maintained this stance as well, at least up until 1936 when the imminent establishment of a Jewish Israel forced him to finally support the desires of his people.[5]

Regarding the first phase of Islam's relationship with the West Aburish writes, "*All political leadership of the time depended on Islam for legitimacy and all political leaders were pro- British. Islam was a tool to legitimize the rule, tyranny and corruption of Arab leaders. To the West, Islam was acceptable; it could be and was used.*"[6]

This phase of elitist domination of the Arab people,

---

[5] Ibid p. 57 and 59

[6] Ibid p. 57

using Islam as the legitimizing factor, could not continue indefinitely. The force that rose up to counter it was secular Arab nationalism and it eventually revolved around the person of Gamal Abd-al Nasser of Egypt. This movement sought to free the Middle East from Western domination and at the same time it was cynical of the Islam that had been used so successfully to prop up and justify elitist rule. We will identify the second phase of Western-Islamic relations that began with the rise of Arab nationalism, but first we must take a brief historical look at Egypt

Peter Goodgame

III. Britain and Egypt

By the beginning of World War I Egypt had been controlled by Britain for more than thirty years. While the British used Islam to topple the Ottomans and prop up their client states outside of Egypt, within Egypt they found that Islam was not such a malleable asset, at least not while Britain remained as the colonizer.

Western influence over Egypt began in 1798, when Napoleon invaded Egypt to threaten Britain's trade routes to India. This was the first major and decisive conquest of an Arab Muslim nation in the history of Islam and marked the beginning of a slow decline in Muslim pride and influence. Napoleon's rule didn't last long, however, because the British temporarily allied with the Ottomans to throw the French out after only a few years.

Out of the chaos emerged an Albanian commander of the Ottoman army named Mohammed Ali, who helped to drive out the British, afterwards becoming governor of Egypt under Ottoman authority. Ali neutralized the native Mamluke threat, and then turned his attention to modernizing Egypt. After Ali died his successors Abbas, and then Said Pasha ruled Egypt. Said Pasha started the Suez Canal, and then his successor Khedive Ismail finished it in 1869. The canal was financed primarily by French investors, but by this time France was firmly controlled by Britain. After that the British influence in Egypt slowly became stronger and stronger, and was initially done not militarily but *economically*. The British "free-trade" ideology was adopted and Egyptian manufacturing and industry suffered. Egypt soon found itself deep in debt.

In 1879 Ismail was forced from power and was eventually succeeded by his son Tewfiq Pasha who finally gave up and effectively ceded complete control of the Egyptian economy over to the British. In 1882 British troops landed and completed the takeover of Egypt. They would occupy Egypt until 1956 when they were finally expelled by President Nasser.

At the beginning of World War I the Khedive Abbas perceived a chance to shake off the British and he urged popular support for the Ottomans. The British quickly deposed him and placed his uncle Hussein Kamil in power. After the war was over nationalist forces within Egypt waged a continuous campaign against the British occupiers for independence, even lobbying for international recognition for independence in Paris, but their desires were dashed when the United States sided with Britain.

In 1922 the British repealed the "Protectorate Status" over Egypt, but they maintained responsibility for Egypt's "defense" and for protection of foreigners within Egypt. Egypt was said to have achieved "independence" and King Fouad I, descendent of Mohammed Ali, took power, although British occupation continued.

In 1928 the "Muslim Brotherhood" was founded by an Egyptian schoolteacher named Hasan al- Banna. The Brotherhood was a religious secret society known publicly for its emphasis on Islamic education and for its charitable activities. Prior to World War II British

Intelligence cultivated ties with the Brotherhood through agent Freya Stark, the British adventurer and writer.[7] These covert connections were used to keep track of the growing German presence in North Africa and to stay informed of the many different political movements that were springing up.

The Muslim Brotherhood spread throughout the Muslim world and has evolved into something like a Muslim equivalent of the West's Masonic brotherhood. It became one of the first Islamic Fundamentalist terror organizations and will crop up often in this study.

In the years prior to World War II Egyptian intrigues revolved around the three main camps of the British, who did all they could to maintain control over their colony and the Suez Canal, the Royalists allied with King Fouad, and after 1935 his son King Farouk, and the nationalist Wafd party that was supported by the people through the Egyptian parliament that had been set up by the British.

When World War II broke out the Wafd party, at least publicly, supported the allies because they were led to believe that complete independence would immediately follow the war. King Farouk, however, was more reserved in his support for the allies and privately held deep axis sympathies, while many rank-and-file members of the Muslim Brotherhood were known to favor Germany as well. Germany was not destined to free Egypt from the British, however, and the axis'

7 *MI6 - Inside the Covert World of Her Majesty's Secret Intelligence Service*, Stephen Dorril, 2000 p. 622

North African army was defeated at the Battle of El-Alamein in October, 1942 and then gradually pushed out of Africa.

After the war both the Muslim Brotherhood and the populist Wafd Party agitated against the repressive monarchy of King Farouk and against the British who delayed their pullout from Egyptian territory. In 1949 Hasan al-Banna was assassinated by the Egyptian government, enraging the fundamentalists even more. In 1952 the Wafd Party won a great victory in Parliamentary elections and in the aftermath Prime Minister Nahas Pasha repealed the 1936 agreement that had been made between Farouk and the British allowing British control of the Suez Canal. Farouk promptly dismissed Nahas Pasha and widespread violent anti-British riots ensued. A secret cabal of high-level Egyptian Army officers, calling themselves the Free Officers, seized this opportunity and staged a coup, taking over the country and throwing out King Farouk.

The Free Officers were led by General Muhammad Naguib and included Gamal Abd-al Nasser and Anwar al-Sadat. In the aftermath Naguib was removed and Nasser emerged as the man in power in 1954. He promptly banned the Wafd Party as well as the Muslim Brotherhood and began to rule as a firm dictator.

Nasser was quick and bold in his moves to modernize and industrialize Egypt and to assert his nation's independence. He reached out to the United States and to the World Bank to help him finance the construction of the Aswan Dam, but he was denied and forced to turn to the Soviets. He also sought to improve his army and was offered Western armaments but on condition that he commit his country to the British-controlled regional military alliances. Nasser declined, and signed an arms deal with Czechoslovakia in 1955.

On July 26, 1956 Nasser evicted the British from the Suez Canal Zone, returning it to total Egyptian control for the first time since 1882. Three months later the Suez War began. Israel took over Gaza in five days and British and French troops took over the Canal Zone. The United Nations condemned the action and a cease fire was agreed to on November 6. The Canal was then returned to Egypt.

In the aftermath of this war Nasser became a hero to the Arab people and secular nationalist movements sprang up throughout the Middle East. Egypt merged with Syria forming the United Arab Republic in 1958, and then (North) Yemen federated with them as well. This pan-Arab movement was loved by the Arab masses but feared by their leaders. Aburish writes,

"In the 1950s and later, the West opposed the secular Arab nationalist movement for two reasons: it challenged its regional hegemony and threatened the survival of its clients leaders and countries. Specifically, there was nothing to stop a secular movement from cooperating with the USSR; in fact, most of them were mildly socialist. Furthermore, most secular movements advocated various schemes of Arab unity, a union or a unified policy, which threatened and undermined the pro-West traditional regimes of Saudi Arabia, Jordan and other client states.

The West saw it as a challenge that had to be met.[8]

This brings us to the second phase of Western-Islamic relations as defined by Aburish. It is a period during which the West used Islamic Fundamentalism as a tool to destabilize or topple the regimes that refused to be dominated by the West.

[8] *A Brutal Friendship - The West and the Arab Elite*, Said K. Aburish, 1997 p. 60

IV.   The Overthrow of Iran's First Democracy

From the beginning America's Central Intelligence Agency has maintained a very close relationship with British intelligence and this is proven by the details of the Mossadegh coup in Iran in 1953, which marked the beginning of the second phase.

Dr. Mohammad Mossadegh was a lifelong leader of the Iranian nationalist movement against the imperialism of the British Empire. Born into Iran's ruling class he was elected to the Iranian parliament in 1906, but turned down the post because, legally, he was too young (being not yet 30). He received his education in France and Switzerland and received his law doctorate in 1913. He returned to Iran and served as a university professor, deputy Finance Minister and Minister of Justice prior to the British-backed coup of 1921 which placed Shah Reza Khan back in power.

In the following years Mossadegh served the Iranian people in a number of different capacities, finally being forcibly removed from public service near the end of Reza Khan's reign due to his criticism of the corrupt regime. In 1941 the government changed again and Reza Khan was forced to flee to South Africa, where he lived until he died. Mossadegh was then able to return to Tehran, where he was active in the Parliament, clashing with Reza Khan's son Mohammad Reza Shah.

After fighting through a great deal of interference and fraud Mossadegh was elected as Iran's Prime Minister by the Iranian Parliament in 1951. On May 1, in one of his first actions as Prime Minister, Mossadegh nationalized Iranian oil, taking it over from the British owned Anglo- Persian Oil Company. The British had bought control of Iranian oil for 60 years, through William Knox d'Arcy, from Reza Khan back in 1901. They purchased another 60-year lease from the Shah again in 1933. After taking control of Iranian oil Mossadegh was forced to campaign at the UN and at The Hague to counter a British lawsuit by arguing that the contracts made with prior governments were not valid. Mossadegh was successful and the international community declared that Iran had every right to take control of its own oil.

Mossadegh's nationalization move was not made without concern for British interests. His government promised to pay 25% of oil profits to the British as compensation and guaranteed the safety of British jobs. Nonetheless, the British refused to negotiate and responded with a show of naval force, followed by economic blockades, boycotts and the freezing of Iranian assets.[9]

Over the preceding years widespread anti-British sentiment had resulted in a greatly decreased intelligence capability for the British within Iran, so to effectively deal with Mossadegh the British turned to their pals in the American CIA. Author Stephen Dorril documents this affair in his book *MI6: Inside the Covert World of Her Majesty's Secret Intelligence Service*. He writes:

---

[9] *Killing Hope - U.S. Military and CIA Interventions Since World War II*, William Blum, 1995 p. 65

"Despite British propaganda, the Mossadeq government was generally democratic, moderate, and seemed likely to succeed in establishing a middle-class hold over the state. It was officially viewed by the Truman administration as popular, nationalist and anti-communist."[10]

To change the American position on Mossadegh British strategists capitalized on America's communist paranoia and tried to portray Mossadegh's regime as weak and a possible avenue for Soviet manipulation. Near the tail end of the Truman administration the head of the CIA's Middle East Department, Kermit Roosevelt, met with John Sinclair and other MI-6 representatives where they *"put to him the proposal that they jointly topple Mossadeq".*[11] After Eisenhower took over the presidency in January of 1953 the CIA was free to act, and American involvement was confirmed when the British promised to allow American oil companies a 40% stake in Iranian oil in return for toppling Mossadegh and re-acquiring Iranian oil reserves.[12]

The British and Americans finally settled on the virtually powerless son of Reza Khan, Mohammad Reza Shah, to be the new ruler of Iran. At first the young Shah turned down the offers made to him by the conspirators, even after visits from American Colonel H. Norman Schwarzkopf on August 1, 1953, and a later meeting with Kermit Roosevelt. Dorril writes that, *"The Shah finally agreed to support the plan only 'after official US and*

---

[10] *MI6 - Inside the Covert World of Her Majesty's Secret Intelligence Service,* Stephen Dorril, 2000 p. 575

[11] Ibid p. 580

[12] Ibid p. 583

British involvement had been confirmed through a special radio broadcast.'" BBC Persia was used to convey a pre-arranged coded message over the airwaves for the ears of the Shah in order to satisfy his doubts.[13]

To prepare for the coup the Americans funded Ayatollah Bihbani and the British gave a group led by Ayatollah Qanatabadi $100,000 to stir up unrest against Mossadegh. Ayatollah Kashani was given $10,000 by the CIA and his followers played a role in the demonstrations in central Tehran. Another group of fundamentalist agitators was led by Tayyeb Hsaj-Reza'i, a figure who later became a supporter of the Ayatollah Khomeini.[14]

In mid-August, 1953, Mossadegh's government was beset by a multitude of CIA and British- funded plots and demonstrations. On August 15 Mossadegh's Foreign Minister was kidnapped in a bid to intimidate the government. On August 16 the Shah issued a statement dismissing Mossadegh as Prime Minister and at the same time propaganda materials were distributed that falsely alleged that religious mullahs were to be hanged by members of the communist Tudeh party.[15] On August 17 and 18 mobs made up of religious fanatics and supporters of the Shah converged on Tehran creating chaos and terror. On August 19, in collusion with the chief of police, the mobs were able to reach the Prime Minister's residence and after a fierce battle Mossadegh was forced from power. Several days

---

[13] Ibid p. 589
[14] Ibid pp. 592-593
[15] Ibid p. 592

later the Shah returned from Italy and thus began his 25-year dictatorial regime. The story of the Shah's downfall twenty-five years later, at the hands of the same fundamentalist fanatics who helped him acquire his throne in the first place, involves the British as well, which we will find out momentarily. Radical Islam was indeed a useful tool for the British, and their manipulation of it was only just beginning.

Peter Goodgame

V.   The British War against Nasser

In their dealings with Nasser the British used any means necessary, including espionage, diplomacy, bribery and even direct military might to retain control over Egypt and the Suez Canal. The newly founded CIA also became interested in Egypt when Nasser showed signs of tilting to the Soviet Union. Aburish explains how this new avenue of intrigue evolved,

"According to CIA agent Miles Copeland, the Americans began looking for a Muslim Billy Graham around 1955... When finding or creating a Muslim Billy Graham proved elusive, the CIA began to cooperate with the Muslim Brotherhood, the Muslim mass organization founded in Egypt but with followers throughout the Arab Middle East... This signalled the beginning of an alliance between the traditional regimes and mass Islamic movements against Nasser and other secular forces."[16]

The CIA was following the example of British Intelligence and sought to use Islam to further its goals. They wanted to find a charismatic religious leader that they could promote and control and they began to cooperate with groups such as the Muslim Brotherhood. With the rise of Nasser the Brotherhood was also courted more seriously by the pro-Western Arab regimes of Saudi Arabia and Jordan. They needed all the popular support that they could muster against the rise of Nasser-inspired Arab nationalism to keep their regimes intact.

---

[16] *A Brutal Friendship - The West and the Arab Elite*, Said K. Aburish, 1997 p. 60-61

The Muslim Brotherhood was an obvious ally against Nasser, because he had abolished it from Egypt after it was involved in a failed assassination attempt on his life in 1954. The Brotherhood rejected Nasser's policy that, for the most part, kept religion out of politics. Officially the Brotherhood was an outlawed organization, but it remained influential and active within Egypt working against the secular regime, often hand-in-hand with British Intelligence. In June of 1955 MI6 was already approaching the Brotherhood in Syria to agitate against the new government that showed strong left-wing tendencies and a desire to merge with Egypt.[17] The Brotherhood became an even more important asset after Nasser announced the Egyptian takeover of the Suez. Author Stephen Dorril documents how this move was viewed from Britain,

"On 26 July in Alexandria, in a calm speech, but one that was described by London as hysterical, Nasser made his nationalisation announcement, which from a strictly legal point of view was no more 'than a decision to buy out the shareholders.' That night in Downing Street, [British Prime Minister] *Eden's bitterness at the decision was not concealed from his guests... Eden summoned a council of war, which continued until 4 a.m. An emotional Prime Minister told his colleagues that Nasser could not be allowed, in Eden's phrase, 'to have his hand on our windpipe.' The 'muslim Mussolini' must be 'destroyed.' Eden added: 'I want him removed and I don't give a damn if there's anarchy and chaos in Egypt.'"*[18]

[17] *MI6 - Inside the Covert World of Her Majesty's Secret Intelligence Service*, Stephen Dorril, 2000 p. 622
[18] Ibid p. 623

Former Prime Minister Churchill had fueled Eden's fire by counseling him about the Egyptians, saying, *"Tell them if we have any more of their cheek we will set the Jews on them and drive them into the gutter, from which they should have never emerged."*[19]

Sir Anthony Nutting, a member of the Foreign Office at the time, recalls an irate phone call from Eden who was upset at the slow pace of the campaign against Nasser. Eden raged, *"What's all this poppycock you've sent me? ... What's all this nonsense about isolating Nasser or "neutralizing" him, as you call it? I want him destroyed, can't you understand? I want him murdered..."*[20]

To prepare the way for the desired coup the British Information Research Department (IRD) was called into action. They ratcheted up their efforts to control radio broadcasts into Egypt and they planted false stories in the BBC, the London Press Service and the Arab News Agency. Forged documents were created that suggested that Nasser was planning to take over the entire Middle East oil trade, and a bogus report was disseminated that alleged that Egyptian dissidents were being sent to a concentration camp manned by ex-Nazis.[21]

The British had a problem though in deciding who would take over Egypt after Nasser's removal. MI-6 held meetings with members of the old Wafd party and

---

[19] *Descent to Suez - Foreign Office Diaries 1951-1956*, Sir Evelyn Shuckburgh, 1986 inside flap
[20] Dorril, p. 613
[21] Dorril, pp. 624-625

allies of former premier Nahas Pasha. The original Free Officer's leader General Neguib, who had been removed and placed under house arrest by Nasser, was viewed as a possible president, and some British circles even advocated that Prince Abdul Monheim, the most 'presentable' Egyptian royal, be made king.[22]

According to Dorril, the most important recruit to the British plot to topple Nasser was an Egyptian Intelligence officer Isameddine Mahmoud Khalil, who was maintained as a contact by supplying him with intelligence about Egypt's most pressing enemy: Israel. Dorril offers a Mossad chief's remarks about this situation who said, *"Harming Israel's security by handing over secret information about her did not apparently trouble the conscience of the British."* This was a very complicated time for the British, because they were presently working *with* Israel to coordinate a military attack on Egypt which eventually took place in October.[23]

Evidently, the lack of a clear-cut candidate to replace Nasser did not stop the coup plotters. Dorril concludes that, *"MI6 did not believe, however, that it was absolutely necessary to have an alternative in place. The Service was confident that once Nasser was overthrown suitable candidates would emerge."*[24]

In late August Nasser acted against the growing threat from British Intelligence. The offices of the Arab News Agency were raided and a number of employees were

[22] Dorril, p. 629
[23] Dorril, p. 629-630
[24] Dorril, p. 630

arrested and confessed to being British agents. Two British diplomats were expelled, one of them, J. B. Flux, had "*been in contact with 'students of a religious inclination' with the idea of 'encouraging fundamentalist riots that could provide an excuse for military intervention to protect European lives.'*" Other British "businessmen" and "diplomats" were arrested or expelled as well, and because of Nasser's effective offensive Dorril writes that immediately prior to the Suez War British Intelligence found that it was left "*With no assets in the country,*" and that "*MI6 had to use outside agents for its assassination plans.*"[25]

In the end all of this British subversion and agitation failed, even after they decided upon the direct military confrontation that was played out in the Suez War of October 1956. Popular Egyptian support for Nasser was just too much, and the international community sided with Nasser against the British as well, forcing the Suez Canal to be returned to Egypt. Nasser emerged leading an Egypt finally free from British control.

Since then Britain has continually waged a low-level covert war against Egyptian governments: against Nasser until his death, against Sadat who took over, and even against Mubarak after him, up until this very day. The secular Egyptian government has traditionally been one of the toughest enemies of Islamic terrorism, whereas the single most important backer of Egyptian terror groups has been Britain. This last statement goes entirely against the preconceptions of most British and American citizens, but in the pages that follow we will offer proof to back it up.

---

[25] Dorril, p. 632-633

Peter Goodgame

VI.   Islam Turns Against the West

As we have related, in his book *A Brutal Friendship*, Said Aburish defined three phases of Western-Islamic relations. The first was the period during which Britain used Islam to help legitimize the puppet dictators that they had installed over their Arab colonies after World War I. The second phase was a period during which Britain (and America) used militant Islam as a force to help topple governments such as Mossadegh's and Nasser's that were trying to fight Western domination. Aburish writes,

"The struggle between Nasser and the Muslim Brotherhood and its offshoots and Western and traditional Arab regimes' supporters continued until the 1967 War. Western support for Islam was provided openly and accepted by the leadership of the Islamic movements without reservation."[26]

Aburish notes that Islam had a good image in the West up to this time. The Islamic movement was noted most for its anti-communist outlook and there was little foresight that conservative Islam might turn against the West. Aburish then begins to describe the third phase,

"The third phase in the development of Islamic movements occurred after the 1967 war. The defeat of Nasser was a defeat for the force he represented, secularism, and with Nasser diminished, the Islamic movements moved to assume the political leadership of the masses of Arab Middle East."[27]

---

[26] Aburish, p. 61
[27] Aburish, pp. 61-62

After 1967 the power of the Islamic movements greatly increased. Islamic theology overtook secularism and a more potent form of Arab nationalism emerged. The Six Day War saw the West stand by as Israel defeated her Arab neighbors, capturing the Sinai, the West Bank and the Golan Heights. It then became clear to most Muslims that the West favored Israel over the Arabs and resentment towards the West increased. This third phase of Western-Islamic relations began when factions of this predominantly anti-Western Fundamentalist Islamic movement began to exercise their new political influence throughout areas of the Muslim world.

After Nasser died in 1970 and was replaced by Anwar al-Sadat the new Egyptian president tried to appease the threat of militant Islam by releasing all of the imprisoned members of the Muslim Brotherhood, despite the fact that the Brotherhood had been involved in at least four separate assassination attempts on Nasser's life over the previous sixteen years. Sadat then joined forces with King Faisal of Saudi Arabia and they became sponsors and promoters of the Al Azhar Islamic University as well as Islamic movements such as Al Dawa and I'tisam. These leaders realized that it was best to at least appear to support the rise of the Islamic movements.[28]

On October 6, 1973 Egypt and Syria launched a surprise attack on the Israeli Army in the Sinai and the Golan Heights. On October 16 OPEC raised the price of oil by a whopping 70%, and then the next day Arab OPEC leaders announced that they would enforce a

---

[28] Aburish, p. 62

progressive embargo against Europe and the United States until Israel was forced to withdraw to their pre-1967 borders.

Engdahl's book, *A Century of War,* relates how US National Security Advisor Henry Kissinger was able to convince Germany *not* to declare neutrality regarding the October war, while Britain *"was allowed to clearly state its neutrality."* Britain remained neutral throughout the entire episode and was one of the few Western countries not placed under the Arab oil embargo.[29]

The Yom Kippur War ended on October 26, but the effects were such that the Arab regimes came out much better in several respects. Firstly, they had finally been effective militarily against Israel and they had won back some territory. Secondly, their regimes were infused with a great deal of popular support and the voice of the Islamic militants was temporarily quelled.

Lastly, the Arab nations suddenly became the benefactors of a huge increase in oil revenues, from $3.01 a barrel in early '73, to $11.65 a barrel in early '74.[30]

Engdahl relates that the rise in oil prices was something that had been planned previously by the Anglo-American Establishment and mentioned at the Bilderberg conference in May, 1973 in Saltsjoebaden, Sweden. Kissinger was the point man in engineering the Arab-Israeli conflict that created the excuse for the oil

[29] *A Century of War*, Engdahl p. 151
[30] Ibid pp. 151-152

price hike that helped to rescue Britain's North Sea oil projects that had previously been seen as risky investments. The most catastrophic effect, however, was that the rise in energy prices put a quick halt to Third World industrialization, forcing many countries to borrow a great deal of money over the years to pay for energy, thus setting the stage for the long-term indebtedness of the Third World to Anglo-American banks.[31] After the war the Establishment awarded Kissinger the Nobel Peace Prize and later he received an honorary knighthood from Queen Elizabeth, for his lifelong devoted service to the Crown, in 1995.

The Arab regimes were suddenly greatly enriched as a result of the rise in oil prices, but the threat of the Islamic movements remained. King Faisal of Saudi Arabia feigned support for Islam, but was often forced to crack down on the religious leaders and organizations that seemed to constantly criticize the royal family's overt greed, luxury and corruption. Faisal was assassinated in 1975 by his nephew Prince Faisali bni Musad, in retaliation for Faisal's execution of Musad's Muslim Zealot brother who had attacked a TV station on the grounds that it was a violation of Islam.[32]

In Egypt Sadat's regime came under extreme pressure from the Islamic movements after he signed the Camp David Accords with Israel in 1978. This led to the assassination of Sadat, by members of Islamic Jihad, an offshoot group of the Muslim Brotherhood, on October 6, 1981.

---

[31] Ibid pp. 150-156
[32] Aburish, p. 62

In Syria, in 1982, there was a major conflict between the Muslim Brotherhood and the Syrian government at the city of Hamma that resulted in 20,000 casualties. In the aftermath Syria's President Asad revealed that the Muslim Brotherhood forces were armed with US-made equipment. Aburish comments on how none of these events seemed to change the way in which militant Islam was used,

"Hamma, the assassination of Sadat and Faisal and less portentous acts didn't interrupt Western and Arab client regimes' support for Islamic movements, and Saudi Arabia and Egypt allowed pro-Islamic use of their state propaganda apparatus... And Israel, forever inclined to back divisive movements, surfaced as another supporter of Islam and began to fund the Muslim Brotherhood and the Palestinian Islamic movement Hamas."[33]

The most noteworthy success of the Islamic movement during this time was of course the overthrow of the Shah of Iran and the installation of the Ayatollah Khomeini as the Islamic dictator. British Intelligence had used their contacts with Iran's *mullahs* and *ayatollahs* to help overthrow Mossadegh and install the Shah back in 1953, and these contacts were maintained and used again to overthrow the Shah when his regime fell out of favor.

The Establishment history of Iran's Islamic Revolution is that Khomeini's revolt was spontaneous and populist, and that it overthrew a repressive dictatorship that was hated by the people but supported wholeheartedly by the United States. It is true that the Shah's government

---

[33] Aburish, p. 62

was not a democracy and that his secret service, trained by the CIA, was one of the most effective intelligence organizations in the world. But what is not reported is that prior to the British- sponsored massive public relations campaign on behalf of the Ayatollah the government of the Shah was loved by the vast majority of the population.

After taking over from Mossadegh the Shah began to push forward a number of nationalist policies that increased his popularity at home but, in some cases, worried the Anglo-American Establishment. First, he signed petroleum agreements with ENI, the Italian oil company. Then in 1963 he pushed forward on a series of popular reforms that became known as the White Revolution. The Shah evolved into a nationalist whose path paralleled that of Nasser far too much for the Establishment's liking:

-       He bought land from the upper classes and, along with the crown's own land, sold it back cheaply to tenant farmers, allowing over one a half million people to become land owners and ending the old feudal system.
-       He allowed women the right to vote, and brought an end to the wearing of the veil, which were "Westernizing" moves unwelcomed by the religious sector.
-       He pushed forward on a $90 billion nuclear power program.
-       He moved to shut down the lucrative opium industry that had been created during the days of

British Empire control that had been running for a hundred years.[34]

In 1973 *The Economist* magazine featured Iran on the front cover with the caption: *"Iran the Next Japan of the Middle East?"* Iran's economy had grown at a rate of 7-8% each year from 1965-1973 and was becoming an example for the developing nations of the world to follow. As far as the Anglo-American Establishment was concerned this could not be allowed to continue. Establishment goals were focused on world de-population and de-industrialization as formulated by policy makers like Lord Bertrand Russell and as advocated by establishment lackeys such as Kissinger, Zibigniew Brzezinski and Robert McNamara (the head of the World Bank), as well as by the British elites who controlled the World Wildlife Fund and other environmental front groups. Iran had to be brought down.[35]

The attack on the Shah's government came through the Muslim Brotherhood and through the mullahs and ayatollahs of Iran, supported and manipulated by British Intelligence. Dr. John Coleman, a former British Intelligence agent and author of a number of books and monographs detailing the Establishment's plan for a socialist world government, states in his report on Iran's Islamic Revolution[36] that the Muslim

---

[34] *Conspirators' Hierarchy: The Committee of 300*, Dr. John Coleman, 1992, p. 129, http://www.sedona.net/pahlavi/mrp.html and
http://www.cbc.ca/news/indepth/iran/iran2.html
[35] *What the Malthusians Say*, Establishment plans to stop Third World development and kill off useless eaters
[36] *What Really Happened In Iran*, Dr. John Coleman

Brotherhood was created by *"the great names of British Middle East intelligence, T.E. Lawrence, E.G. Browne, Arnold Toynbee. St. John Philby and Bertrand Russell,"* and that their mission was to *"keep the Middle East backward so that its natural resource, oil, could continue to be looted..."*

Dr. Coleman writes that in 1980 the broadcasts of Radio Free Iran divided the enemies of the Shah into four categories:

    1. Iranian politicians bought by the Israeli Shin Bet,

    2. The CIA's network of agents,

    3. The feudal landowners,

    4. The Freemasons and the Muslim Brotherhood (viewed as the same enemy).

In his report Dr. Coleman writes that in Iran, *"At one time there was even a joke about the mullahs being stamped 'made in Britain.'"* When the Shah introduced his plan for modernization in 1963 the Ayatollah Khomeini emerged as the leader of the religious opposition. Up until his exile from Iran in 1964, Khomeini was based at the religious city of Qom. Dr. Coleman relates that Radio Free Iran claimed that while at Qom Khomeini received a *"monthly stipend from the British, and he is in constant contact with his masters, the British."*

Khomeini was kicked out of Iran and settled in Iraq. He lived there for a number of years until he was arrested by the Iraqi government and deported in 1978. French President D'Estang was then pressured to offer Khomeini refuge in France to continue his "Islamic studies." While in France he became a Western celebrity and the symbol of the anti-Shah Islamic revolution.

Coleman writes, *"Once Khomeini was installed at the Chateau Neauphle, he began to receive a constant stream of visitors, many of them from the BBC, the CIA and British intelligence."*

At the same time Amnesty International was continuing its intense campaign against the Shah's government, accusing it of torture and other terrible human rights abuses. The international press picked up on this theme and carried it around the world.

The BBC then became the Ayatollah's main promoter. Dr. Coleman writes, *"It was the BBC, which prepared and distributed to the mullahs in Iran all of the cassette tapes of Khomeini's speeches, which inflamed the peasants. Then the BBC began to beam accounts of torture by the Shah's SAVAK to all corners of the world... In September and October 1978 the BBC began to beam Khomeini's inflammatory ravings direct to Iran in Farsi.* **The Washington Post** *said, 'the BBC is Iran's public enemy number one.'"*

The BBC Persian Service came to be nicknamed in Iran the "Ayatollah BBC" for its non-stop coverage of everything that Khomeini wanted to say.[37] Soon a large segment of the Iranian public, most of them impressionable young students, became convinced that the Shah truly was evil and that a return to pure *shi'ite* Islam under the Ayatollah's leadership was the only way to save their country. The Carter Administration, manipulated by British lackey Zbigniew Brzezinski, then collaborated with the British to topple the Shah and install Khomeini.

---

[37] *BBC Persia brings down two Iranian regimes*, and *The BBC In Iran*

Dr. Coleman relates that Carter appointed Trilateralist George Ball to head a commission on U.S. policy in the Persian Gulf. Ball's recommendation was that the U.S. should withdraw its support for the Shah's regime. Dr. Coleman quotes from the Shah's own memoirs to confirm the American stance, the reality that is contrary to the mass-marketed Establishment line that the U.S. supported the Shah to the end,

"I did not know it then, perhaps I did not want to know - but it is clear to me now, the Americans wanted me out. What was I to make of the sudden appointment of Ball to the White House as an advisor to Iran? I knew that Ball was no friend of Iran. I understood that Ball was working on a special report on Iran. But no one ever informed me what areas the report was to cover, let alone its conclusions. I read them months later when I was in exile, and my worst fears were confirmed. Ball was among those Americans who wanted to abandon me, and ultimately my country."

After the Shah stepped down in 1979 and fled the country his "firm ally," the United States, even refused to allow him asylum forcing him to move with his family to Egypt. During the subsequent takeover of the American embassy when supporters of the Ayatollah kept Americans hostage for 444 days it became crystal clear to the entire world that the anti-democratic, anti-Israel Islamic movement was also very anti-West. Nonetheless the Anglo-American Establishment continued to support and promote radical Islam.

In 1977 Bhutto of Pakistan, who we will cover shortly, was removed; in 1979 the Shah of Iran was removed; in 1981 Sadat was assassinated, and in 1982 the Muslim

Brotherhood revolted in Syria. Before 1977 the Middle East was on the verge of achieving stability and industrial and economic parity with the West through nationalist policies and high oil prices, but by the early '80s the Middle East was in flames. Egypt was reeling and Mubarak was consolidating a shaky hold on power. Iran and Iraq, both armed by the West, were beginning their long war. Israel and Syria were invading Lebanon that was fighting a civil war, and Russia was invading Afghanistan whose rebels were being supported by Pakistan. The de-population and de-industrialization scheme advocated by the British and adopted by the Americans was off to a great start.

VII. Afghanistan, Pakistan, the ISI and the BCCI

On July 3, 1979, at the insistence of advisors such as Zbigniew Brzezinski, President Carter signed a directive authorizing covert aid to the fundamentalist opponents of the ruling communist regime in Afghanistan.[38] This move was understood as one that would likely lead to direct Soviet intervention and that is exactly what happened on December 24 of that year when, after being invited by the Afghani government, the Russian military took up positions to protect government assets from rebel attacks.

From the beginning of the Afghan War the CIA partnered with Pakistani Intelligence (ISI) and funded the rebel *mujahedin* fighters. Today it is generally understood that radical Islam received its biggest boost as a result of the mujahedin's successful *jihad* against Soviet forces, and when the Soviets retreated from Afghan territory in early 1989 the country was left with tens of thousands of unemployed Islamic mercenaries who then turned their attention to the West.

The history of Afghanistan has always been closely connected with Pakistan, a region formerly colonized by Britain. British involvement in the subcontinent goes back as far as the early years of the seventeenth century when British East India Company merchants were allowed to establish trading posts by the the Emperor Jahangir of the Islamic Mughal Empire. Direct British

---

[38] *Interview with Zbigniew Brzezinski*, Le Nouvel Observateur

rule in India is generally seen as beginning in 1757 when BEIC forces led by Robert Clive defeated the army of the Nawab of Bengal at the Battle of Plessey. In 1803 British control over the subcontinent increased even further when the rulers of the Mughal Empire became pensioners of the BEIC. The Indus River Valley, the center of modern Pakistan, was brought under British control through the successful campaign of 1848-1849 that conquered the Sikh empire, giving the British the Punjab. Since then the regions that are today India and Pakistan were ruled by Britain continuously until the British Empire withdrew and created the two nations in 1947.

When Britain withdrew a number of British officers remained behind to help shepherd (and control) the emerging Pakistani Army. One of these was Major General Walter Joseph Cawthorn who, as Deputy Chief of Staff of the Pakistani Army established Pakistan's Inter-Services Intelligence (ISI) in 1948. Cawthorn was an Australian-born British Intelligence (MI-6) agent who had directed operations in the Middle East, Indian, and Southeast Asian bureaus from 1939- 1945. He became Sir Cawthorn in 1958 when he was knighted by the British Crown, and later he served in Australia as head of their Secret Intelligence Service.[39] Pakistan's ISI was originally a military intelligence agency created to help defend Pakistan in the early wars against India over Kashmir and other border issues, but over the years it has grown to become Pakistan's version of the CIA,

---

[39] *First Supplement to A Who's Who of the British Secret State*, LOBSTER magazine, May 1990 Pakistan's Inter-Services Intelligence in Afghanistan, SAPRA INDIA, *There to the Bitter End*, Anne Blair

and it has continually maintained close ties with British Intelligence.

The power of the ISI increased for its first twenty years until the emergence of Pakistan's first popularly elected civilian leader, the socialist Zulfikar Ali Bhutto in 1971. Bhutto immediately displayed the same nationalistic characteristics as Nasser, Mossadegh and the Shah and his regime fell out of favor with the British government and the West. In 1972 Bhutto withdrew his country from the British Commonwealth of Nations and he pursued closer relations with Russia, China and the Arab states.

In 1977 the inevitable coup took place, and President Bhutto was overthrown by General Zia Ul-Haq, who had been appointed to Chief of the Army Staff by Bhutto in 1976 at the insistence of Gulam Jilani Khan, the longstanding Director General of the ISI. Bhutto comments at great length on his constant struggles with, and betrayal by, the ISI in his book *If I Am Assassinated,* penned from his Pakistani prison cell. He also relates how Kissinger threatened him for pushing forward on Pakistan's nuclear power program, telling him, *"We will make an example of you!"* He was. Bhutto was executed in 1978 after being subjected to a sham trial, despite the objections of heads of state from around the globe.[40]

A radical spokesman of the Muslim Brotherhood had this to say several years later, *"The Brotherhood has taken*

---

[40] Zulfikar *Ali Bhutto biography,* ppp.org *ISI and its Chicanery in Exporting Terrorism,* by Maj Gen Yashwant Deva, The Indian Defence Review

over in Iran and Pakistan. Bhutto stood for intrusion of the West into Islam. Bhutto was everything that Pakistan was not. That is why we killed him. And we will use his death as a warning to others.[41]

Britain's relation with the Pakistan underworld becomes clear with a look back at the BCCI scandal. The **Bank of Credit and Commerce International** was the first Third World multinational bank, created in 1972 by Pakistani banker Agha Hasan Abedi. It was initially funded by Sheik Zayed of Abu Dhabi, and from a $2.5 million operation it grew to be worth $23 billion when it was finally shut down in 1991. It was created just in time to take advantage of the river of cash that was flowing into the Middle East through the oil industry.

One of BCCI's early moves to gain international influence was its purchase in 1976 of 85% of the Banque de Commerce et Placements (BCP) of Geneva, Switzerland. After the BCCI took over this bank it installed Alfred Hartmann as manager. Hartmann then became the chief financial officer for BCC Holding and thus one of BCCI's most influential directors. Hartmann was a member of the British banking establishment through his connections with the Rothschild family, being a member of the board of directors of N.M. Rothschild and Sons, London, and president of Rothschild Bank AG of Zurich.[42]

BCCI was initially incorporated in Luxembourg, famous

---

[41] *What Really Happened In Iran*, Coleman, p.16, 1984 World In Review, 1-800-942-0821

[42] *The Real Story of the BCCI*, Bill Engdahl and Jeff Steinberg, EIR, 10-13-95

for its lax banking restrictions, and soon branches and holding companies sprouted up around the globe: in the Cayman Islands, the Netherlands Antilles, Hong Kong, Abu Dhabi, Washington DC and just about everywhere else. However, by 1980, when the BCCI finally applied for and received a license from the Bank of England, there were already more branches in the UK than in any other nation. In fact, one of BCCI's primary economics advisors was the former British Prime Minister (1976-79) Lord James Callaghan.[43] The BCCI may have been created by a Pakistani, but in the end it was a British-based and British-controlled bank.

Over the years the BCCI became involved in just about every type of illicit transaction that a bank could be involved in including drug money laundering, weapons dealing, bribery, fraud, etc. It was used extensively by the CIA throughout its history, it played a part in the Iran-Contra scandal, it was a bank used by the Medellin Colombian cocaine cartel, and a branch was even set up in Panama for the cash that Manuel Noriega was funneling out of his country. After BCCI was shut down the UK's *The Guardian* newspaper reported that the terrorist Abu Nidal had maintained BCCI accounts. Jonathan Beaty and S.C. Gwynne, the *Time* reporters who covered the scandal write,

"According to The Guardian's *sources, the Nidal group had long used a London branch of BCCI to move the money it used to mount attacks on Western targets, and MI5 -- the English equivalent of the CIA -- had known about the accounts. There*

---

[43] *The Outlaw Bank: A Wild Ride Into the Secret Heart of BCCI*, Beaty and Gwynne, p. xv

seemed to be no doubt that the BCCI bankers knew exactly who they were dealing with: One of the bankers at the London branch described how anxious they had been to provide every service to the terrorists in order to keep their multibillion-dollar accounts.'[44]

However, the main purpose of the BCCI, and the reason behind its meteoric rise, was its connection to the ISI and the mujahedin fighting the Soviet Union in Afghanistan. After Zia replaced Bhutto as Pakistan's president he appointed his friend Fazle Haq to be the governor of Pakistan's North-West Frontier Province in 1978. This is the area that borders Afghanistan through which tons of drugs and weapons were smuggled over the Khyber Pass. Fazle Haq was an important friend and backer of BCCI's founder Abedi, and the BCCI was used to launder untold millions of ISI narcotics revenues.[45]

Coincidentally, in 1983 the British-based World Wide Fund for Nature (WWF) suggested that two national parks be created in Pakistan's northwest, and although rather thin in natural wildlife the preserves proved to be excellent for poppy growing and for staging mujahedin incursions into Afghanistan.[46]

Former Senate investigator Jack Blum said this about the BCCI's connection to the Afghan war during his

---

[44] Beaty and Gwynne, p. 118

[45] Beaty and Gwynn, pp. 48-49

[46] *"Sadruddin Aga Khan: Mujahideen Coordinator,"* Scott Thomspon and Joseph Brewda, EIR, 10-13-95. The WWF has been used and abused by British Intelligence since its inception in 1961, as documented by British investigative journalist Kevin Dowling. See related article and stories by Dowling in *Noseweek* magazine.

testimony to the U.S. Congress,

"This bank was a product of the Afghan War and people very close to the mujahideen have said that many Pakistani military officials who were deeply involved in assisting and supporting the Afghan rebel movement were stealing our foreign assistance money and using BCCI to hide the money they stole; to market American weapons that were to be delivered that they stole; and to market and manage funds that came from the selling of heroin that was apparently engineered by one of the mujahideen groups."[47]

When General Zia took over Pakistan all of the pieces were in place to begin the massive drug running, fraud and swindling operation that was the Afghan War. According to Beaty and Gwynne, Zia already had a *"close and cooperative relationship"* with BCCI founder Agha Hasan Abedi when he took power[48]. The triangle of General Zia's government, the ISI (who had empowered Zia) and the BCCI then proceeded to run the Afghan *mujahedin* uprising for the CIA, with input from above from British Intelligence. Over the course of the Afghan war up to $5 billion of American taxpayer aid was funneled into the war effort, and through the duration Pakistan's ISI trained about 83,000 Muslim mujahedin fighters.

Britain's role in promoting the Afghan experiment was crucial, although now it is often overlooked. Almost immediately after the Soviet invasion of Afghanistan

---

[47] *"The Real Story of the BCCI,"* Bill Engdahl and Jeff Steinberg, EIR, 10-13-95 10.

[48] Beaty and Gwynn, p. 146, also pp. 251, 262, 279, 286-7, 324, 346

Lord Nicholas Bethell, a career British Intelligence
agent, formed Radio Free Kabul as a voice for the
mujahedin.

Bethell had been involved with Russian and Mid-East
operations his entire career, and he was a close friend of
British spy Kim Philby. Other members of Radio Free
Kabul included Winston Churchill III, former Foreign
Secretary Baron Chalfont, Lord Morrison of Lambeth
the former head of the Foreign Office, and British
Intelligence official Ray Whitney. In 1981 Lord Bethell
accompanied Prime Minister Margaret Thatcher on a
tour of the U.S. to drum up support for the resistance,
and together they met with over 60 congressmen and
senators, eventually leading to the creation of the US-
based Committee for a Free Afghanistan which
continually lobbied in support of the mujahedin.[49]

Another British creation was Afghan Aid UK, first set
up in Peshawar, Pakistan by the wife of British
journalist John Fullerton. This group's primary sponsor
was Britain's Viscount Cranbourne, who later testified
before the U.S. Congress Special Joint Task Force on
Afghanistan to lobby for US support. His organization
was granted substantial funding by the British
government and by the U.S. Agency for International
Development (USAID).

Britain lobbied to create a war in Afghanistan, they
wanted American taxpayers to pay for it, and they
manipulated the financial situation so that they might

---

[49] *The Anglo-American Support Apparatus Behind the Afghani Mujahideen*, Adam
K. East, EIR, 10-13-95

profit from it. The BCCI was shut down by the Bank of England in 1991 only *after* the Russian withdrawal, and only then because of the courageous campaigning of a handful of American investigators. Beaty and Gwynne write,

"Though the Bank of England had pulled the trigger on BCCI on July 5, 1991, and had thereby started a global chain reaction that had smashed Agha Hasan Abedi's brainchild into tiny pieces, it had done so only reluctantly and only after waiting an extraordinary amount of time. It had been cowardly rather than heroic; it had moved only when forced to do so by a formidable U.S. alliance between the Federal Reserve Bank and the Manhattan district attorney."[50]

The final U.S. congressional report on the BCCI affair states,

"By agreement, the Bank of England had in effect entered into a plan with BCCI, Abu Dhabi and Price Waterhouse in which they would keep the true state of affairs at BCCI secret in return for cooperation with one another in trying to avoid a catastrophic multibillion-dollar collapse.

From April 1990 forward, the Bank of England had now inadvertently become partner to a cover-up of BCCI's criminality."[51]

BCCI was the favored bank for Middle Eastern terrorists and arms and drug runners, South American drug cartels, organized crime lords, and even for intelligence services such as the ISI, Mossad, MI6 and

---

[50] Beaty and Gwynne, p. 101
[51] Beaty and Gwynne, p. 106

the CIA. In fact then-CIA assistant director Robert
Gates once referred to BCCI jokingly as the "Bank of
Crooks and Criminals".[52] For at least a decade British
authorities allowed it to run amuck out of their living
room and after it's fall important records were sealed
away and kept from American investigators. When the
scandal broke the media backlash focused primarily on
BCCI's American links and the CIA, but only because
of the British establishment's secrecy and expertise in
damage control. It's likely that the whole truth will
never be known.

As the war in Afghanistan wound down and the
Russian withdrawal became inevitable, the situation
became much more complex. American support for the
mujahedin dropped off as the CIA tried to resist the
establishment of a fanatical Afghani government. New
warlords emerged and other avenues of drug smuggling
were increasingly utilized, through Iran and through the
southern Soviet republics. The dwindling supply of U.S.
Government money and arms, coupled with a
decreasing supply of drug cash, helped along the BCCI
decline.

This brings us to focus on the drug industry and the
impact it has had in shaping Afghanistan. Peter Dale
Scott, Alfred W. McCoy and Michael C. Ruppert are
three authorities in this area. In brief, the conclusion
reached by the experiences and research of these men is
that drugs (most notably cocaine and heroin) are
controlled commodities, just like oil, gold and

---

[52] Beaty and Gwynn, p. 346, and "*The BCCI Affair*," overview and key
documents

diamonds, with intricate Western-supported systems of production, distribution and cash flow. Today the global drug industry generates about $600 Billion a year, and the vast majority of this cash is funneled (laundered) into Anglo-American banks and/or Wall Street. These researchers *allege* that one of the most important tasks of Western intelligence services has been to make sure that the flow of drug cash back into the Anglo-American financial system continues unimpeded. (And yes, the London-based BCCI was, for all intents and purposes, an Anglo-American bank.)

Whatever the case may be, it is worth pointing out that when Britain and the CIA became involved in Afghanistan the production of opium skyrocketed. From an estimated harvest of only 100 tons per year in the early seventies, opium production went up to 300 tons in 1982 and then to 575 tons in 1983. By the late eighties, near the end of the war, Afghani opium poppy production had reached an estimated 1600 tons per year.[53]

The CIA's drug racket was so successful that by 1981 Afghanistan supplied about 60% of America's heroin from contributing an almost negligible amount just two years previously. The crops were grown in Afghanistan, synthesized into heroin in labs on both sides of the Pak- Afghan border, and then smuggled into the US and Europe. General Zia's government was drowning in a sea of heroin as well, despite the international accolades he was receiving for simultaneously reducing the poppy crop on *his* side of the border, and Pakistan's

---

[53] *Opium History, 1979 To 1994* Alfred McCoy

heroin-addict population grew from about 5,000 in 1981 to over 1.2 million by 1985.[54]

It is also worth noting that the US-led war on the Taliban regime occurred after one of the most successful poppy-eradication programs ever seen. In July of 2000 Mullah Omar placed a ban on poppy growing and by February of 2001 UN drug control officials were able to confirm that poppy production had come to a virtual standstill in Taliban-controlled areas. Was the expected loss of drug-revenue an added incentive for the West to remove the Taliban? Does this explain why Afghan farmers have had little resistance in their quick return to their favorite cash crop after the Taliban's demise?[55]

When the CIA became involved in Afghanistan they were almost entirely dependent on their ISI contacts within Pakistan for intelligence and for guidance in directing the war effort. As the war evolved American support was channeled, at the behest of the ISI, to a group of seven independent Afghani mujahedin warlords who became known as the *Peshawar Seven*.

Eventually one of the seven, a warlord by the name of Gulbuddin Hekmatyar, emerged as the primary recipient of American aid, despite his communist past, his radical view of Islam and his blatant anti-Americanism. Hekmatyar had been an engineering student at Kabul University, and then he had trained at

---

[54] *Drug Fallout*, Alfred McCoy, and Pakistan's statement to the UN regarding drug trafficking
[55] *The Lies About Taliban Heroin*, Michael C. Ruppert, FTW

the Kabul Military Academy before being kicked out. Hekmatyar became affiliated with the Muslim Brotherhood in the early '70s, and by the time of the Afghan war he had emerged as the leader of a group called Hezb-i-Islami, or Party of Islam, even though he had never received a classical Islamic education. Over the years his followers became known for their strict Muslim fanaticism (they were notorious for throwing acid on the faces of women who refused to wear a veil), and Hekmatyar became Afghanistan's biggest opium producer. He possessed thousands of acres of poppy fields and, according to McCoy, he owned at least six heroin laboratories on the Pakistan side of the Khyber Pass.[56]

In March of 1990 the US House Republican Research Committee of the Task Force on Terrorism and Unconventional Warfare submitted a 19-page report that criticized the CIA for its dealings with Hekmatyar's "Party of Islam" and for covering up the problems that his group had created. Over time it has emerged that Hekmatyar was an ISI asset who laundered his money through BCCI, and also cooperated with the Russian KGB to ensure his status as the most powerful warlord among many rivals. Jeffrey Steinberg of EIR sums it up,

"Although American diplomats and intelligence officers posted in Pakistan often warned of Hekmatyar's strong anti-western and pro-Iranian views, speculated about possible Soviet KGB links, and even acknowledged his undisputed status as Afghanistan's

---

[56] Blum, pp. 338-352 and *Osama Bin Laden - A CIA Creation and its 'Blowback'*, Mike Ruppert citing McCoy regarding Hekmatyar's six labs, and *Gulbuddin Hekmatyar Had Links With KGB*, Imran Akbar

"heroin king," his forces received the largest portion of American and other international military support throughout the Afghan War. Intelligence reports back to Washington about the progress of the war were notoriously biased, and filled with disinformation portraying Hekmatyar's mujahideen as the most successful fighters. Often the reports to the Pentagon and the CIA were identical to the reports prepared by British intelligence - complete with the same spelling and typographical errors. More reliable on-the-scene reports indicated that Hekmatyar spent more time and effort fighting rival mujahideen groups than battling the Soviets."[57]

The ISI's spin on the situation comes through in the book *Afghanistan: The Bear Trap,* in which Brigadier Mohammed Yousaf, the former head of the ISI's Afghan Bureau, (co-written with a former British Army officer), describes Hekmatyar as *"scrupulously honest"* and the toughest and most vigorous mujahedin leader. Yousaf was the ISI's director of the mujahedin and he argues that the war was drawn out longer than necessary because the United States did not give Hekmatyar and the Islamists *enough* support, which began to fade in the late '80s while the Soviets still occupied Afghanistan. Yousef resents the fact that the CIA did not give the Islamists an overwhelming victory, even though the Taliban eventually emerged after several years of civil war.[58]

Yousef's point of view can be compared to the 1990 US House Republican Report which is covered in this

---

[57] *War In Afghanistan Spawned A Global Narco-Terrorist Force*, Steinberg, 10-13-95 EIR

[58] Yousef, pp. 40-41, 233-235

article by journalist Imran Akbar of *The News International*, which also details the suspected KGB links maintained by Hekmatyar.

After the Taliban took power Hekmatyar was forced to flee to Iran. In February of this year the Iranian government shut down his operations in Iran and expelled him back to Afghanistan.

Hekmatyar has been as outspoken as ever in his anti-American views, offering reward money for the killing of American troops and calling the new US-installed Afghan government illegitimate. In May the CIA reportedly tried to assassinate him with a missile fired from an unmanned Predator drone as he and his entourage journeyed near Kabul. This ISI favorite remains one of the most dangerous players in Afghanistan today.[59]

In his book Yousef also goes to great lengths to make it clear that American personnel were never involved in training any of the Afghan mujahedin,

"Up to the Soviet withdrawal from Afghanistan in early 1989, no American or Chinese instructor was ever involved in giving training on any kind of weapon or equipment to the Mujahideen.

Even with the heavier and more sophisticated weapons systems... it was always our Pakistani teams who trained the Mujahideen. This was a deliberate, carefully considered policy that we steadfastly refused to change despite mounting pressure from the CIA, and later from the US Defense Department, to allow them

---

[59] *"CIA 'tried to kill Afghan warlord,'"* BBC, May 10, 2002

*to take it over. From the start the Americans wanted to be directly involved with the distribution of the weapons, <u>the operational planning of operations</u> and the training of guerillas. From the start, until the last Soviet soldier quit the country, **we successfully resisted**."* [emphasis added][60]

Other than being financier and armament supplier, the American CIA was out of the loop. It was Yousef's ISI that ran the Afghan jihad against the Soviets, and it was the ISI that channeled CIA support to the most undesirable Afghan warlords. What becomes clear after reviewing the record of this era is that the ISI's agenda, and that of the Afghan War in general, was set to a far greater degree by the British than it was by the CIA. The British had formulated and promoted the plan for American involvement; they maintained close relations with the ISI that ran the war; they controlled the bank that largely benefited from it; and when the war was over they welcomed into Britain the many mujahedin veterans who applied for British asylum.

Osama bin Laden was one of these veterans and in early 1994 he purchased an estate and lived for a short while in the London suburb of Wembley. During his time in London he established his **Advice and Reformation Committee** to oversee his economic network, and he solidified his propoganda links to the Western world through his connections with London's Sheikh Omar Bakri and with Abdel Bari Atwan, the editor of *al-Quds al-Arabi*, one of the most influential Arabic-language newspapers in the world. Yossef Bodansky, author of the best-selling biography of bin

---

[60] Youssef, p. 115

Laden writes that, "*By the time bin Laden left London, he had consolidated a comprehensive system of entities with a solid - though clandestine- source of funding. This London-based data-dissemination system still works efficiently.*" (Written in 1999).[61]

---

[61] Bodansky, pp. 101-102

VIII. Further Information

From Executive Intelligence Review:

http://www.larouchepub.com/

Put Britain on the List of States Sponsoring Terrorism

Who Really Controls International Terrorism?

Why the Real Name is 'Osama bin London'

*Bernard Lewis: British Svengali Behind Clash of Civilization*s,
by Scott Thompson and Jeffrey Steinberg

War In Afghanistan Spawned A Global Narco-Terrorist Force,
by Jeffrey Steinberg

From the Middle East Media Research Institute

http://www.memri.org/

Sheikh Omar Bakri Mohammed - London, another member
of the Muslim Brotherhood

Islamist Leaders In London Interviewed

Egyptian Muslim Brotherhood Presents New Suicide Bombers

From the BBC

UK is 'Money Launderers Paradise'

FBI Highlights UK Terror Suspects

Other Sources

The British Connection, by Hichem Karoui

Britain's dissident community of Arab Islamists is a hotbed of radicalism, by Nicolas Pelham

Islamic Militants Have Base In London, Newsday.com

London Seen As Hub For Radicals, USATODAY.com

UK Recruiting Ground for Al-Qaeda, The Times of India

Peter Goodgame

The Muslim Brotherhood: The Globalists' Secret Weapon

I.   The Roots of Islamic Terrorism

Over the past half-century religion has been in decline in the Western part of the world and in most of the East as well. Spirituality has been traded for materialism as living standards have increased, and popular culture has become almost completely secular as well. Why has the situation been different within the Middle East? How come the Judeo-Christian ethic has eroded, but the Islamic ethic has experienced an apparent resurgence? This study will try to explain how this situation is not something that has occurred by chance and it will offer evidence that militant Islam has been a card played by the global elites of the dominant Anglo-American establishment to achieve the long-term goal of a world government.

Before we turn to the events of September 11 we must first look at the small group of Muslim scholars who developed the ideology, and then as we continue it will become clear how tight- knit and closely connected the movement really is. It is a small movement within the religion of Islam, but it is very influential and its effectiveness must be measured in other ways than simply counting the number of adherents to its philosophy.

As we related in **Part One**, the British used Islam to legitimize their puppet rulers in Jordan, Iraq, Saudi

Arabia and Palestine after taking over the Middle East in World War I. Because of this Islam was seen by much of the Arab populace as just another part of the corrupt colonial establishment. That is why the legitimate anti-colonial movements, such as those of Nasser, Mossadegh and Bhutto, were primarily secular in nature. When these nationalist movements began to succeed outside of the British sphere of influence the British turned to their Islamic allies to subvert these independent regimes. The Muslim Brotherhood stands out as the most important counter-revolutionary movement of this period in the Middle East, and one of the British-based Globalists' most important strategic assets today.

The Muslim Brotherhood emerged out of Egypt in 1928 to evolve into *"the largest and most influential Sunni revivalist organization in the 20th century."* It was founded by Hasan al- Banna, the first son of a respected sheik who was also an author and the leader of a local mosque. Hasan was born in 1906 and was brought up immersed in Islam under his father's tutelage. He memorized the Koran and at age twelve he founded an organization called the Society For Moral Behavior. Shortly after he created another group, the Society for Impeding the Forbidden. He was a devout Muslim dedicated to his faith and at age sixteen he enrolled in an Islamic school in Cairo to train to become a teacher. As a teenager Hasan al-Banna also became a member of a Sufi order, the Hasafiyya Brothers' order. He was active in the order, reading all of the Sufi literature he could get his hands on, and he organized a Sufi group, the Hasafiyya

Society for Welfare.[62]

In Part One of this study we related several allegations that the Muslim Brotherhood was created, infiltrated, or at least promoted by British Intelligence and/or British Freemasonry. Dr. John Coleman alleges that it was created by *"the great names of British Middle East intelligence..."*, Stephen Dorril writes that the Brotherhood was linked to British Intelligence through dame Freya Stark prior to World War II, and the Shah's regime in Iran considered it to be a tool of British Freemasonry.

Some Muslims will find these claims hard to believe but they should not be rejected out of hand. Hasan al-Banna was a devout Muslim who put Islam first but it should not be considered inconceivable that he was influenced by Britain's Masonic Brotherhood, or that he accepted British aid to advance his movement, at least in the early stages. Islam was used effectively by the British outside of Egypt, so why would they not try to use it in Egypt as well?

Freemasonry appeared in Egypt soon after Napoleon's conquest in 1798 when General Kleber, a French Mason and top commander in Napoleon's army established the Lodge of Isis. French Masonry dominated Egypt until British lodges began to appear after the British occupation in 1882. Freemasonry was very popular in the first half of the twentieth century, and many important Egyptians were Masons, along with the British rulers and aristocrats who occupied the

---

[62] Biography of Hasan al-Banna

country. In fact the Egyptian monarchs, from Khedive Ismail to King Fouad, were made honorary Grand Masters at the start of their reigns. From 1940 to 1957 there were close to seventy Masonic lodges chartered throughout Egypt. At one time the leaders of the Nationalist and Wafd parties were Freemasons, and many members of the Egyptian parliament were Masons as well, where they mingled with the military commanders and aristocrats of the ruling British occupation.[63]

Two very important Islamic leaders in Egypt, Jamal al-Din al-Afghani and Mohammed Abdou, were also Freemasons. Al-Afghani was a foreigner who had been the prime minister of Afghanistan before becoming an activist in Iran and Russia prior to his appearance in Egypt. He is considered *"the founder of the political pan-Islamic movement,"* and his movement is known as the **Salafiyya** movement. He agitated against British imperialism but at the same time he advocated modernization for the Muslim world. Before being expelled from Egypt he became an important figure at Al-Azhar University in Cairo and his most important disciple was Mohammed Abduh. Throughout his life he was an activist for Muslim self-determination, but several times he visited London where, according to one biographer, *"he reestablished ties with his lodge members."* When al-Afghani died in 1897 he left behind a large body of political and religious writings that would form part of the basis for the later Islamist movements.[64]

---

[63] Freemasonry In Egypt, Insight Magazine, March 1, 1999
[64] Biography of Jamal al-Afghani

After al-Afghani was expelled from Egypt in 1879 Mohammed Abduh continued to promote his reformist message. For this Abduh was expelled in 1882. During his exile he met up with al- Afghani in Paris where they collaborated to publish a Muslim journal and where they expanded their contacts within the Masonic Brotherhood. Four years later the British had a change of heart and they allowed Abduh to return. He became a teacher at Al-Azhar University where he focused on reforming the prestigious Islamic institution. At the same time he quickly rose to become a judge in the National Courts. Only eleven years after returning from his British-imposed exile the ruling British governor, Lord Cromer, made Sheikh Mohammed Abduh the Grand Mufti of Egypt, in 1899. He was now the Pope of Islam.[65] At the same time he was the Masonic Grand Master of the United Lodge of Egypt.[66]

There was of course an ulterior motive for Cromer making Abduh the most powerful figure in all of Islam. You see, in 1898 the ruling council of Al-Azhar University had reaffirmed that usury, and thus banking according to the Western model, was *harem* (illegal) according to Islamic Law. This was unacceptable to Lord Cromer because his given name happened to be Evelyn Baring - he was an important member of England's prestigious Baring banking family that had grown rich off of the opium trade in India and China. Lord Cromer installed his friend Sheikh Abduh to change the law forbidding banking, and once he was

---

[65] Biography of Mohammed Abduh
[66] Commentary from Shaykh Abdul Hadi of the Italian Muslim Association

71

made Grand Mufti he used a very liberal and creative interpretation of the Quran to fabricate a loophole that allowed the forbidden practice of usury. British banks then had free reign to dominate Egypt. In Lord Cromer's writings he says, *"I suspect my friend Abduh was in reality an agnostic,"* and he commented on Abduh's Salafiyya movement saying, *"They are the natural allies of the European reformer."* Even Cromer saw that the Islamist movement could be used to Britain's advantage.[67]

Sheikh Mohammed Abduh had two students that were important in continuing the Salafiyya movement after he died in 1905. One of them was Sheikh Ahmad Abd al-Rahman al-Banna, who was Hasan al-Banna's father. The other was Mohammed Rashid Rida, a freemason who became Sheikh Abduh's good friend and publisher of the monthly magazine, *The Lighthouse*. This mouthpiece of the Salafiyya movement was first published in 1897, and Rida remained the publisher for thirty-seven years. Rida also existed within the British circle of influence and his publication reflected the British point of view by agitating against the Ottoman Empire. He praised the freemasonic Young Turk movement, but after World War I he castigated Turkey's nationalist revolution under Ataturk.[68]

Hasan al-Banna's young life was influenced by all of these factors: by the Islamic movement, by the British occupation, by his father, and by his most important mentor, Mohammed Rashid Rida. Al-Banna grew up

[67] Excerpt from *"The Return of the Khalifate"* by Shaykh Abdalqadir as-Sufi
[68] Biography of Hasan al-Banna; Dietl, p. 26; Dreyfuss, p. 139-140

reading Rida's publication and through his family connections they became good friends. At his death in 1935 Rida had placed all of his hope for an Islamic resurgence in al-Banna's Muslim Brotherhood. The other factor in Hasan al-Banna's life was Freemasonry. Al-Banna experimented with numerous religious sects and political groups as a young man and he also became a member of the Masonic Brotherhood. This was entirely normal for someone growing up in the higher echelons of Egyptian society at the time and his membership was not considered a betrayal of Islamic values as it is today.[69]

In 1927, at the age of twenty-one after graduating from his university, he was appointed to teach Arabic at a school in Ismailiyya. This town happened to be the capital of the British-occupied Canal Zone and the headquarters of Britain's Suez Canal Company. Hasan al-Banna established the Muslim Brotherhood there a year later. The Suez Canal Company helped to provide the funds for the first Muslim Brotherhood mosque that was built in Ismailiyya in 1930.[70]

An important question is how, among a multitude of competing Islamic organizations, did the Muslim Brotherhood expand with such great leaps and bounds to number over 500,000 active members only a decade later? Al-Banna was only twenty-two when it began, and it was based in the heart of British occupied territory for its first four years. Contemporary histories credit the

---

[69] Commentary from Shaykh Abdul Hadi of the Italian Muslim Association
[70] Dreyfuss, p. 143

Brotherhood's success directly to the organizational skills of al-Banna:

The single most important factor that made this dramatic expansion possible was the organizational and ideological leadership provided by al-Banna. He endeavored to bring about the changes he hoped for through institution-building, relentless activism at the grassroots level and a reliance on mass communication. He proceeded to build a complex mass movement that featured sophisticated governance structures; sections in charge of furthering the society's values among peasants, workers and professionals; units entrusted with key functions, including propagation of the message, liaison with the Islamic world and press and translation; and specialized committees for finances and legal affairs. In anchoring this organization into Egyptian society, al-Banna skillfully relied on pre-existing social networks, in particular those built around mosques, Islamic welfare associations and neighborhood groups. This weaving of traditional ties into a distinctively modern structure was at the root of his success.[71]

The bottom line is that the Muslim Brotherhood's success could not have been achieved without the approval of the British ruling establishment, and al-Banna's association with the Masonic Brotherhood goes far to explain how efficiently it was organized and how seamlessly it fit into Egyptian society. Like the Masonic

---

[71] Biography of Hasan al-Banna

Brotherhood it was established initially as a charitable organization. However, while Freemasonry was liberal and allowed members of all faiths to join, the Muslim Brotherhood was focused specifically on Islam. It was Masonry for Muslims only. Like Masonry the Muslim Brotherhood was devoted to secrecy and it was run according to a pyramidal command structure. The foot soldiers at the bottom had no idea of the true goals of the leaders at the top.

The Muslim Brotherhood was established with the approval and the support of the British establishment, but such a popular mass movement proved hard to control. The Egyptian people harbored a deep anti-British resentment, and this feeling inevitably dominated the Muslim Brotherhood. It ceased to be solely a charitable and religious organization in the late 1930s when it entered the realm of politics to support the Palestinian Arab uprising against the British and the increasing influx of Jewish immigrants. Anti-British activity soon began to pick up within the Brotherhood back at home, and early in World War II al-Banna was briefly imprisoned by the pro-British regime for allowing his organization to get out of hand.

After World War II ended al-Banna found that he was one of the most powerful leaders in Egypt. He found himself in a struggle for power against the monarchy and the secular Wafd party, and his organization was seen as the most militant, the most radical and the most dangerous. In 1948 members of the Muslim Brotherhood were implicated in the assassination of the police chief of Cairo and the government retaliated when Prime Minister Nuqrashi Pasha issued a proclamation in December of 1948 dissolving the Muslim Brotherhood. Its headquarters and branches were shut down and its assets and funds were seized. Hundreds of members were arrested and incarcerated and the Muslim Brotherhood was driven underground. Weeks later Nuqrashi Pasha was assassinated by the Brotherhood, and then on February 12, 1949 Hassan al-Banna was himself assassinated by Egypt's secret police.

In May of 1950 the government tried to reconcile with the Brotherhood and released most of the captured members from prison. The next year the ban on the Brotherhood was repealed, but it was forced to maintain itself under a new law passed to regulate the many different Egyptian societies, groups and organizations.

As the monarchy continued to decline in popularity, moving way too slowly to break away from Britain for the public's liking, two subversive groups schemed behind the scenes to control Egypt's destiny: the Free Officers and the Muslim Brotherhood, the army and the fundamentalists. The army proved to have the upper hand, especially after the death of al-Banna, and Nasser finally emerged as the man to lead Egypt on an independent path. At first the Brotherhood supported the army and attempts were made to include them in the new government, but the Brotherhood over-estimated its strength and influence and demanded too much. Then after Nasser won his power struggle with General Naguib the Brotherhood knew that it faced a tough future. Nasser was far less understanding of the fundamentalists than was Naguib and the break became complete after the Brotherhood attempted to assassinate Nasser in October of 1954. Many years later the deposed and embittered General Naguib claimed in his memoirs that the assassination was a sting operation planned by Nasser to make an excuse to do away with the troublesome Brotherhood once and for all.[72]

In any case, by the end of 1954 thousands of Brotherhood members were imprisoned, including almost all of its leaders, and six were executed. It was this break that paved the way for a new relationship between the Muslim Brotherhood and the intelligence services of Britain and America because all of them were united in their hatred of Nasser. Unfortunately for the West the Brotherhood remained largely ineffective within Egypt throughout Nasser's reign, even though they were involved in several more attempts on his life. During this time many fleeing members were welcomed in London, where they set up a presence that remains to this day, and a number of them also relocated in Syria, Jordan and Saudi Arabia.

Hasan al-Banna created an organization described by Arab historians as *"the greatest modern Islamic movement."* Al-Banna was known to say:

"We need three generations for our plans - one to listen, one to fight, and one to win."[73]

He died young at the age of 43. His was the "listening" generation, but he was the speaker. After his premature death several other leaders emerged to continue to

[72] Dietl, p. 56
[73] Dietl, p. 32

instruct the believers within militant fundamentalist Islam.

One of them was a man by the name of Sayed Qutb. He eventually became recognized as the *"chief ideologist"* of the Muslim Brotherhood after al-Banna, and his extensive writings justify the beliefs of radical Islamists today. Muslims rarely take the radical path of Islam without reading something written by Qutb.

Sayed Qutb was the same age as al-Banna, and also a Freemason, but he did not even join the Brotherhood until after al-Banna's death. He had become critical of the West after living in the United States for a time and when he returned to Egypt he embraced fundamentalism. He advanced within the Brotherhood very quickly and served as their ambassador in Syria and Jordan before becoming the editor of the Brotherhood's official periodical in 1954. However, upon the "assassination attempt" of Nasser he was arrested with many of his compatriots, cruelly tortured and then sentenced to fifteen years in a labor camp. One year later a representative from Nasser offered him amnesty if he would but ask for forgiveness. Qutb refused and remained in prison, studying and writing on Islam's role in the modern world. He developed the doctrine that according to Islam, modern Arab states such as Egypt are overrun by *Jahiliyyah*, which is a term translated as *barbarity*, primarily pertaining to the influence of Western culture and political systems. Qutb wrote:

"It is not the function of Islam to compromise with the concepts of Jahiliyya which are current in the world or to co-exist in the same

land together with a jahili system... It derives its system and laws and regulations and habits and standards and values from a source other than Allah. On the other hand, Islam is submission to Allah, and its function is to bring people away from Jahiliyyah towards Islam. Jahiliyyah is the worship of some people by others; that is to say, some people become dominant and make laws for others, regardless of whether these laws are against Allah's injunctions and without caring for the use or misuse of their authority. Islam, on the other hand, is people's worshipping Allah alone, and deriving concepts and beliefs, laws and regulations from the authority of Allah, and freeing themselves from the servitude to Allah's servants. This is the very nature of Islam and the nature of its role on earth. Islam cannot accept any mixing with Jahiliyyah. Either Islam will remain, or Jahiliyyah; no half-half situation is possible. Command belongs to Allah, or otherwise to Jahiliyyah; Allah's Shari'ah will prevail, or else people's desires...[74]

Qutb believed that Arab states governed by anything other than Islamic *Shariah* law were compromised by *Jahiliyyah*, and he advocated the violent use of force to overthrow political systems, especially Nasser's regime in Egypt, in order to eradicate *Jahiliyyah*. Qutb wrote, "The *foremost duty* of Islam is to depose Jahiliyyah from the leadership of man."[75]

In 1964 Qutb was pardoned and released at the insistence of the visiting Iraqi head of state. Qutb then published perhaps his most important work, a book entitled *Milestones*. Nasser used the militant language within the book as an excuse to incarcerate Qutb once

---

[74] Excerpt from *The Right To Judge*, by Sayed Qutb
[75] Excerpt from *The Right To Judge*, by Sayed Qutb

again. At the same time, fearful of a re-organized Brotherhood plot against his regime, Nasser rounded up 20,000 other suspected Brotherhood members as well. On August 29, 1966 Nasser made an example out of Sayed Qutb and executed him by hanging.

Over the course of Sayed Qutb's life he published 24 books, as well as a 30-volume commentary of the Koran. Today his work inspires fundamentalist Muslims within Egypt and around the world and his life is held up as an excellent Islamic example of how to carry oneself in the face of persecution and hardship.

Another of the "speakers" for the first generation of revolutionary Islamist militants was Mustafa al-Sibai. He was born in Syria and educated at the preeminent Islamic university of Al-Azhar in Cairo, Egypt. It was there that he became involved with the Muslim Brotherhood. He was imprisoned for a time by the British, and then after he returned to Syria he was arrested and imprisoned again for his constant revolutionary activities, this time by the French. In 1946, after serving his sentence, Mustafa al-Sibai formed the Society of the Muslim Brotherhood of Syria as a branch subordinate to the Egyptian base.

Al-Sibai's career in Syria was eventually quite successful. He completed his doctorate in Islamic law and began teaching Arabic and religion in Damascus. In 1951 he married into a powerful Damascus family. He traveled throughout the West, published books, gave lectures and helped to direct the Muslim Brotherhood until his death in 1964.[76] Al-Sibai was one of the most articulate spokesmen of the Islamic movement and he had a great understanding of what was happening in the Middle East. In one of his many articles he wrote about Western business interests in Arab lands:

They are the direct reason for foreign intervention into the domestic matters of the country and are the great obstacle toward the realization of independence and dignity. On the one hand, the [oil] concessions are the legacy from the Turks; on the other hand, the concessions were granted under the veiled assertion that it would be economically good for the country and the people. But history has shown that such firms constitute the beginning of colonialism.[77]

The father of Pakistan's Islamic movement is considered to be Abul Ala Maududi. Born in 1903 he first achieved influence in 1937 when he became the director of the Islamic Institute of Research in Lahore. When Pakistan was made a nation in 1948 he objected to the secular nature of the British-sponsored government and for this he served time in jail in 1948 and again in 1952. Maududi's lasting achievement, along with his eighty published books and brochures, is his organization **Jamaat-e Islami**, or **Islamic Society**. Maududi and his group maintained close links with the Muslim Brotherhood and Dietl writes that, *"Both organizations still consider themselves branches of the same movement. At times the Muslim Brotherhood even recognized*

---

[76] Dietl, pp.37-39
[77] Dietl, p. 38

Maududi as the legal successor to its ideologists al-Banna and Sayed Qutb."[78]

Maududi is well known for his articulation of the ideal Islamic state, and his definition is accepted by the majority of Muslims within the militant Islamist movement. In the following passage he comments on democracy:

The difference between Islamic democracy and Western democracy is, of course, the following: while the latter is based on the conception of the sovereignty of the people, the former is based on the principle of the caliphate [leadership] by the people. In Western democracy, the people are sovereign; in Islam, sovereignty rests with God, and the people are his caliphs or subjects. In the West the people themselves make the law; in Islam the people must follow and obey the laws that God communicated through his prophets. In one system the government carries out the will of the people; in the other the government and people together must translate God's intentions into deeds. In short, Western democracy is a kind of absolute authority that exerts its power freely and in an uncontrolled manner, whereas Islamic democracy is subject to the divine law and exerts its authority in harmony with the commands of God and within the framework established by God.[79]

---

[78] Dietl, p. 42
[79] Dietl, p. 43

The last of the revolutionary Islamic ideologists that we will focus on is an Iranian by the name of Ali Shariati. Here is another concrete connection between the Islamic movement and Freemasonry, because Ali Shariati was himself a Mason. His father, Muhammad Taqi Shariati, was a Mason as well who was also, at least at one time, an agent for the far eastern division of British Intelligence.[80]

Ali Shariati was born in 1934. He went to school in Mashad and grew up in the shadow of his father who led a revolutionary Islamic center called the **Center for the Propagation of Islamic Truth**. After Prime Minister Mossadegh was overthrown and the Shah took over Ali Shariati joined the **National Resistance Movement**. In 1957 he was arrested with his father and a handful of other activists and spent six months in prison.

The Shariati family had powerful friends in high places and Ali was accepted to the prestigious Sorbonne University in France. He began his studies there in 1960, receiving a doctorate in sociology and Islamic history. While in France he was exposed to, and captivated by, a group of elitist intellectuals known as the *Existentialists*. This was a group of anti-capitalist and anti- materialist writers that included Jean-Paul Sartre, Frantz Fanon, Albert Camus, Jacques Berque, Louis Massignon and Jean Cocteau. Shariati also developed a fine appreciation for many Marxist ideas.

---

[80] Dreyfuss, pp. 106-108 (excerpt); *What Really Happened In Iran*, Dr. John Coleman, 1984, p. 24

Shariati returned to Iran in 1965 and was immediately arrested. He was known to have been involved with groups that sought to overthrow the Shah while he was in France, and he had helped to create the Iranian National Front for Europe. However he was immediately released, and he subsequently took up a teaching job near Mashad. For the next five years he focused on writing, promoting his view of Islam and cultivating ties with the Muslim Brotherhood and other resistance groups.

In the early 1970s Dr. Shariati began to give lectures on politics and religion, publicly promoting his writings and pushing his views that were diametrically opposite to those of the Shah, who was developing industrial infrastructure, advancing economic development and advocating modern secular education. Shariati wrote, *"Come friends, let us abandon Europe, let us cease this nauseating, apish imitation of Europe. Let us leave behind this Europe that always speaks of humanity but destroys human beings wherever it finds them."*[81]

Ayatollah Khomeini would have never been successful were it not for Shariati's constant agitation against the Shah, done under an intellectual guise and focused on the students and fundamentalists of Iran. For a time Shariati was considered the most influential speaker in Tehran's forums. Dietl writes:

Shariati's importance shows that the Iranian revolution was fostered not only by the old mullahs and ayatollahs, but also by agitated youth who to

[81] Dreyfuss, pp. 106-108

some extent were influenced by other models. As many as 5,000 listeners attended the public lectures given by Shariati. His writings were distributed in the hundreds of thousands, although arrest and torture were the penalty for owning them. Often, the modest, quiet Shariati spoke all day and then held discussions late into the night. After he had given more than 100 lectures, SAVAK [secret police] tried to arrest him, but Shariati escaped; he gave himself up to the police only after they had seized his father as hostage. For two years he was gruesomely tortured in Komiteh prison.

After his release he was not permitted to indulge in any teaching activities or to maintain any conspiratorial contacts. The secret police followed every move.[82]

Finally in 1976 Ali Shariati was able to make an escape to London and there while waiting to catch a plane to meet up with members of his family in the United States he died of a brain embolism. The usual allegation, now almost universally accepted, is that SAVAK agents assassinated Shariati with the use of a poison needle dart dipped in cobra poison. The fact remains that although the Shah hated Dr. Shariati and the repressive philosophies he advocated the cause of Shariati's brain embolism has never been proven.

Hasan al-Banna predicted three generations before the Islamic movement would take over the Middle East. He said that the first generation would demand "listeners"

---

[82] Dietl, p. 45

and he, Sayed Qutb, Mustafa al-Sibai, Abul Ala Maududi, and Ali Shariati were a few of the most prominent strategists laying the ideological groundwork for the modern Islamist movement. The next generation was predicted by al-Banna to be a generation for "fighting."

II.   Creating the 'Arc of Crisis'

By the 1970s elitist intellectuals and globalist institutions had focused on population growth and industrial development as two of the most pressing enemies of the human race. The United Nations, the Club of Rome, the Tavistock and Aspen Institutes and many other organizations that served as mouthpieces for the ruling elites all began crying out that the environment was being destroyed and that industrialization was becoming a terrible menace. Technology, science and human progress were falling out of favor. The elites considered the earth's resources their possessions and they did not want to share them with an emerging and developing Third World.

Lord Bertrand Russell was one of the most important of these anti-human "humanists" who advocated a return to the dark ages. He believed that, *"The white population of the world will soon cease to increase. The Asiatic races will be longer, and the negroes still longer, before their birth rate falls sufficiently to make their numbers stable without help of war and pestilence. Until that happens, the benefits aimed at by socialism can only be partially realized, and the less prolific races will have to defend themselves* **by methods which are disgusting even if they are necessary***."*

Russell was also an advocate for world government, *"I have already spoken of the population problem, but a few words must be added about its political aspect. .... It will be impossible to feel that the world is in a satisfactory state until there is a certain degree of equality, and a certain acquiescence everywhere in the power of the World Government, and this will not be possible* **until the poorer nations of the world have become**

Peter Goodgame

*... **more or less stationary in population.** The
conclusion to which we are driven by the facts that we have been
considering is that, while great wars cannot be avoided until there
is a World Government, a World Government cannot be stable
**until every important country has nearly stationary
population.***" For Russell, population control was a
prerequisite to World Government.[83]

As far back as 1947, a leading Australian scientist was
suggesting, in a secret report to the Australian Defence
Department, that "...the most effective counter-offensive to
threatened invasion by overpopulated Asiatic countries would be
directed towards the **destruction by biological or
chemical means of tropical food crops** and the
dissemination of infectious disease capable of spreading
in tropical, but not under Australian, conditions." This
archetypical mad scientist was Sir Frank MacFarlane
Burnet, knighted by the British crown in 1951, and
winner of a Nobel Prize in 1960.[84]

In 1968 Stanford biologist and Bertrand Russell admirer
Paul Ehrlich wrote the best-selling book **The
Population Bomb**. He wrote, "A cancer is an uncontrolled
multiplication of cells; the population explosion is an uncontrolled
multiplication of people.... We must shift our efforts from the
treatment of the symptoms to the cutting out of the cancer. **The
operation will demand many apparently brutal and
heartless decisions.**" In his book he advocated placing
birth control chemicals into the world's food supplies.[85]

---

[83] Russell quotes from "Malthusians" above
[84] "Nobel winner supported biological warfare as form of population control," from
The Interim, April '02
[85] "Malthusians"

Sir Julian Huxley, the British scientist and intellectual who played a leading part in creating the United Nations Educational, Scientific and Cultural Organization (UNESCO), held much the same views. He saw scientific advancement, such as penicillin, DDT and water purification, as a two-edged sword. He wrote, *"We can and should devote ourselves with truly religious devotion to the cause of ensuring greater fulfillment for the human race in its future destiny. And this involves* **a furious and concerted attack** *on the problem of population; for the control of population is…a prerequisite for any radical improvement in the human lot."*[86]

Huxley's extremist views have remained within the United Nations and they were showcased in the world's first Earth Summit, the Stockholm Conference on the Human Environment in 1972. Maurice Strong was chosen to put together this conference by UN Secretary General U Thant, and the next year Strong was put in charge of the newly created UN Environment Program.

1972 was also the year in which the Club of Rome published their infamous report *Limits to Growth.* This report, backed by research done by the Massachusetts Institute of Technology, basically concluded that industrialization had to be halted to save the planet from ecological catastrophe. Since then even the Club's most loyal admirers, such as Maurice Strong, have admitted that the report was "premature," and didn't take into account advances in technology.[87]

---

[86] Julian Huxley, "Essays of a Humanist," 1964
[87] Strong, p. 119

The Club of Rome has been one of the most influential groups promoting world government since it was created in 1970 by Dr. Alexander King, a British scientist and diplomat, and Arelio Peccei the Italian industrialist. In 1973 the Club published a report entitled *Regionalized and Adaptive Model of the Global World System*, that presented a model of a one world government system sub-divided into ten regions.

The *Aspen Institute* is another important globalist think tank. It was established in 1949 by three Chicagoans: a businessman, the president of the University of Chicago and one of his professors. The University of Chicago was founded with Rockefeller money, and the Aspen Institute has always existed within the Rockefeller sphere of influence. One of the high points of the history of the Aspen Institute was a conference on *"Technology: Social Goals and Cultural Options"* in 1970 that paved the way for the UN's Earth Summit in Stockholm in 1972.

The World Wildlife Fund is another elitist racist institution that masquerades as a humanitarian environmentalist organization. It was created by Prince Phillip of England, the husband of the Queen. He is on record as saying that if he is reincarnated he would like to return as a killer virus, to help solve the overpopulation problem. Since then other WWF executives have voiced the same concerns about overpopulation.[88]

Dr. Arne Schiotz, a WWF director has said, *"Malthus*

---

[88] "Malthusians"

has been vindicated, reality is finally catching up with Malthus. The Third World is overpopulated, it's an economic mess, and there's no way they could get out of it with this fast-growing population. Our philosophy is: back to the village."

Sir Peter Scott, former chairman of the WWF warned, *"If we look at things causally,* **the bigger problem in the world is population**. *We must set a ceiling to human numbers. All development aid should be made dependent on the existence of strong family planning programs."*

Thomas Lovejoy, a former vice-president of WWF put it bluntly, ***"The biggest problems are the damn national sectors of these developing countries. These countries think that they have the right to develop their resources as they see fit. They want to become powers."***

These repressive views are held even by some of the most important managers of the global financial institutions. Fritz Lutweiler, the chairman of the Bank for International Settlements (the world banking headquarters), has said, *"It means* **the reduction of real income in countries where the majority of the population is already living at the minimum existence level or even under it.** *That is difficult, but one cannot spare the highly indebted countries this difficult path. It is unavoidable."*[89]

Robert McNamara, the president of the World Bank warned, *"There are only two possible ways in which a world of 10 billion people can be averted. Either the current birth rates*

---

[89] "Malthusians"

must come down more quickly. Or the current death rates must go up. There is no other way. There are, of course, many ways in which the death rates can go up. In a thermonuclear age, war can accomplish it very quickly and decisively. Famine and disease are nature's ancient checks on population growth, and neither one has disappeared from the scene.... To put it simply: **Excessive population growth is the greatest single obstacle to the economic and social advancement of most of the societies in the developing world.**"[90]

Ultimately these views became accepted within the American foreign policy establishment. In 1974 Secretary of State Henry Kissinger submitted National Security Study Memorandum 200 (NSSM 200) entitled, "*Implications of Worldwide Population Growth for U.S. Security and Overseas Interests.*" The conclusion:

"*World population growth is widely recognized within the Government as* **a current danger of the highest magnitude** *calling for urgent measures.... There is a major risk of severe damage [from continued rapid population growth] to world economic, political, and ecological systems and, as these systems begin to fail, to our humanitarian values.*"

NSSM 200 was to have been made public in 1979, but it was successfully kept under wraps until 1989. During his career Kissinger made sure that population control remained a cornerstone of his foreign policy strategy, and after him his ideological partner Zbigniew Brzezinski pushed the same agenda in the Carter administration. Both are closely connected with the Rockefeller family, and both had studied under

90 "Malthusians"

Harvard's William Yandell Elliott, the Oxford-trained British-allied professor.

The WorldWatch Institute was created in 1974, during the same time that NSSM 200 was being promoted in America's foreign policy establishment, with a grant from the Rockefeller Brothers Fund. Since 1984 its annual *"State of the World"* publication is always highlighted by the media, and its hundreds of alarmist pseudo-scientific papers and reports have been used as ammunition in the leftist and elitist war against industrialization ever since.

As we related in Part One of this study, the first attack on the Third World came in the form of a premeditated massive rise in oil prices in connection with the Yom Kippur war of 1973. Economies cannot develop without an energy supply, and the quadrupling of energy prices was a major setback to nations like India, Brazil, Pakistan, Indonesia and Mexico. Then when President Bhutto of Pakistan tried to work around the situation by developing nuclear energy Kissinger threatened him saying, *"We will make an example of you!"*[91]

The Shah of Iran, even though his nation had an abundant supply of oil, also began a program to develop nuclear energy. Both leaders were quickly eliminated.

With the rise in energy prices the development of the Third World was checked, but the Arab Middle East became greatly enriched. This was when the Globalists

---

[91] Biography of Zulfikar Ali Bhutto

turned to their allies, the Islamists, to remedy the situation. Islam would be used to attack industrialization and modernization using the lie that human progress was un-Islamic and a *Western* plot against the servants of Allah. The real plot was actually aimed at the brown-skinned masses of the Middle East who were briefly experiencing a positive change in their quality of life in terms of education, employment, shelter, sanitation and nutrition. However the religious and intellectual advocates of ignorance, filth and violence joined forces to throw the prosperous Middle East back into the dark ages.

In England the **Islamic Foundation** was set up as a branch of the *Jamaat-e Islami* by Professor Kurshid Ahmad in Leicester in 1973. When General Zia took over Pakistan he appointed Ahmad to serve as his Minister of Economics.[92] Also in 1973 the **Islamic Council of Europe** was created with headquarters in London. The Council's long-time Secretary General was a prominent Muslim Brother by the name of Salem Azzam, who we will return to later.[93]

Another project was **"Islam and the West,"** begun at Cambridge in 1977 with Muslim Brother and former Syrian prime minister Maarouf Dawalibi in collaboration with the Club of Rome's Peccei and Britain's Lord Caradon, along with Dr. Alexander King's **International Federation of Advanced Study.** "Islam and the West" assembled a policy outline effectively defining Islam as a backwards religion in a

---

[92] Dietl, p. 72
[93] Islam in the British Isles, a timeline

struggle with science and technology. The Globalists were determined to promote only the repressive anti-Western minority version of Islam and the Muslim Brotherhood was the key to selling this view to the world.[94]

In Iran members of the Aspen Institute and the Club of Rome linked up directly with the ideological opponents of the Shah's regime in Iran. Ali Shariati, Abolhassan Bani-Sadr and many of the leading educators in Iran's universities were brought into their circle of influence. The Globalists' destabilization campaign against the Shah is documented in Robert Dreyfuss' book *Hostage to Khomeini*, of which a portion can be read at the website dedicated to Iran's former Prime Minister Amir Abbas Hoveyda.

Crucial to the overthrow of the Shah was the Iranian branch of the Muslim Brotherhood known as the **Fedayeen-e Islam**, which had been set up in the 1940s. It was led by the fanatical Ayatollah Khalkali, and the Ayatollah Khomeini was a longtime member. The students who took over the American embassy in Tehran after the overthrow of the Shah, taking scores of American hostages, were also members of the Fedayeen-e Islam. Khalkali was able to personally exercise his political power during the Iranian revolution when he presided as judge in the trials of thousands of political prisoners, sentencing the majority of them to death.[95]

---

[94] Dreyfuss, excerpt
[95] Dreyfuss, pp. 72-83

The Fedayeen-e Islam also controlled Iran's opium production and drug smuggling network which, near the end of the Shah's reign, had become increasingly threatened by the Shah's largely successful anti-dope campaign. After Khomeini took over Khalkali was cynically made head of Iran's national anti-drug program and under his watch opium production skyrocketed. According to Khomeini's rulings, since collected and translated into English, *"Wine and all other intoxicating beverages are impure, but opium and hashish are not."*[96]

In Pakistan the Muslim Brotherhood in the form of the Jamaat-e Islami supported the overthrow of Prime Minister Zulfikar Ali Bhutto by General Zia ul-Haq. Bhutto was hated by the British globalists for withdrawing Pakistan from the British Commonwealth, for implementing nationalistic policies, for leaning towards the Soviets and for seeking to develop nuclear energy. When General Zia announced a death sentence on the imprisoned Bhutto his sentence was officially protested by the heads of state from fifty-four countries. Zia went ahead and executed Bhutto in 1979 only after receiving assurances from the head of the Jamaat-e Islami that the execution would not lead to internal unrest.[97] In the years that followed the Jamaat-e Islami became Zia's most important backer and the nation was forced into a brutal process of Islamization.

In Afghanistan the CIA, prodded on by British Intelligence, began to fund the Islamic opponents of

[96] Dreyfuss, pp. 92-95
[97] 1979 in Pakistan history (see April 3)

the pro-Soviet regime even prior to the Soviet invasion. President Carter's National Security Advisor Zbigniew Brezinski advocated the subversion in order to *provoke* the Soviet invasion that occurred on December 24, 1979.[98] General Zia and the Jamaat-e Islami in Pakistan were two crucial elements that made the mujahedin revolt in Afghanistan successful. Their takeover of Pakistan was a necessary part of the plan to pull the Soviets into the Afghan conflict. As related in Part One, an Afghan warlord affiliated with the Muslim Brotherhood by the name of Gulbuddin Hekmatyar emerged as the primary recipient of American military aid, despite his well-known anti-Western views and his radical view of Islam.

(When the US Congress finally acted to put an end to this aid it was already too late. Hekmatyar reached the pinnacle of his success in 1993-1994 and also in 1996 when he served as Afghanistan's prime minister. He was eventually driven out of Afghanistan by the Taliban but today he is back, agitating against the new government of Hamid Karzai. In May of 2002 the British took it upon themselves to patrol the area where Hekmatyar was based in Operation Buzzard. The stated goal was the suppression of Hekmatyar's forces, but Hekmatyar remains at large and his forces have been suspected in recent terrorist bombings in Kabul. Perhaps the stated goal of Operation Buzzard was not the real goal.)

In Egypt the Muslim Brotherhood experienced a resurgence after President Sadat began to loosen

---

[98] Interview with Brzezinski

restrictions against the organization in the early '70s. Publicly the Muslim Brotherhood attempted to soften its image into that of a "moderate" Islamic organization, but behind the scenes it spawned off a number of violent extremist groups. Islamic Jihad, the Islamic Group and Takfir wal Hejra are just a few of the interlinked terrorist groups that began to agitate more openly against Sadat after he signed the historic Camp David peace agreement with Israel in 1978. Militants associated with these groups assassinated Sadat in 1981 and martial law was declared as the new leader, President Mubarak, launched a vigorous crackdown on the Islamists.

In Syria the Muslim Brotherhood revolted against the Assad regime and took over the city of Hamah. The Syrian government's siege against the Brotherhood stronghold lasted for three weeks. 6,000 soldiers and 24,000 civilians were killed in the intense fighting and in the aftermath 10,000 more residents were arrested and placed in internment camps. Afterwards the Syrian government showed evidence that the Muslim Brotherhood forces had been armed by the West.

This explosion of violence throughout the Middle East in the late '70s and early '80s was referred to by Zbigniew Brzezinski as the **"Arc of Crisis."** It was not something that occurred by chance, but was in fact the result of the deliberate plan developed by the Globalist strategists such as Dr. Alexander King, Henry Kissinger, Zbigniew Brzezinski and British operative Dr. Bernard Lewis. The Middle Eastern "Arc of Crisis" was not a spontaneous internal conflagration, it was something that came about as a result of Western policy in league with the Muslim Brotherhood. Without help from the West radical Islam would have remained the illegitimate, repressive minority movement that it has always been, and the Middle East would have remained stable and prosperous.

III.   The Muslim Brotherhood Branches Out

At the beginning of World War II the Muslim Brotherhood gained a huge amount of prestige when it was joined by members of the influential Azzam family of Egypt. Abdel-Rahman was the most famous of these Azzams, and his whole life had been one of service to the British Empire. After World War I he had worked with British Intelligence to help organize the political work of Libya's Senussi Brotherhood.[99] His work was very successful and the head of the Senussi Brotherhood was proclaimed king of Libya at a UN ceremony in 1951. (At first a darling of the British Empire, King Idris I led Libya until being ousted by Moammar Khaddafi in 1969. Khaddafi's own revolutionary organization had been established in London in 1966,[100] but his regime quickly fell out of favor with the British.)

After World War II Abdel-Rahman Azzam became the first Secretary-General of the British- sponsored **League of Arab States**. Azzam's prestige is proven by the fact that his daughter Muna was married to Mohammed, the eldest son of King Faisal of Saudi Arabia.[101]

In 1955 after General Nasser cracked down on the

---

[99] *Hostage to Khomeini* Dreyfuss, p. 133
[100] *Libya: history*,
http://gbgm-umc.org/country_profiles/country_history.cfm?Id=71
[101] *Biography* of Ayman al-Zawahri:
http://www.fas.org/irp/world/para/ayman.htm

Muslim Brotherhood the organization moved its base of operations to London and Geneva. The Geneva base was under the control of Said Ramadan, who was married to the daughter of Hasan al-Banna. Ramadan set up the **Institute for Islamic Studies** and under his control Geneva became a major Islamic base in Europe. Today this is where King Fahd of Saudi Arabia flees to anytime he feels that his life is in danger back in the kingdom. The following story demonstrates Ramadan's intimate connections to the worldwide Islamist underground:

Soon after the Iranian revolution a man named Ali Akbar Tabatabai became the most important voice of opposition to the Ayatollah's regime. Under the Shah he had been information counselor at the Iranian embassy in Washington D.C. and after the Shah's fall he had set up the Iran Freedom Foundation. In July of 1980 he was murdered by David Belfield, also known as Daoud Salahuddin. Belfield was a Black Muslim who was part of a gang connected with Bahram Nahidian who was reputed to be the Washington head of the Ayatollah's secret service (Savama). Less than two hours after the murder Belfield placed a person-to-person call to Said Ramadan in Geneva, and then using several different passports he fled the United States bound for Switzerland.[102]

Geneva has always been a useful base for the Muslim Brotherhood but its London headquarters became the most important. The man in charge there is Salem Azzam, a relative of Abdel- Rahman Azzam. As

---

[102] Dreyfuss, pp. 174-175

previously mentioned, he became the head of the Islamic Council of Europe that was formed in London in 1973 in close collaboration with Said Ramadan. Dreyfuss explains the role of the Council, **"[the Council] directs the Ikhwan [Brotherhood] from Morocco to Pakistan and India, controlling hundreds of 'religious' centers across Western Europe, and through them, thousands of fundamentalist students and Muslim clergy in both the Middle East and Europe."**[103]

In 1978 the **Islamic Institute for Defense Technology** was created to support the Islamic "arc of crisis" revolution. The inaugural seminar was held in London in February of 1979. It was to work hand in hand with NATO, and it was led by Salem Azzam and members of his Islamic Council of Europe. Pakistan and Afghanistan were at the top of the agenda and the IIDT helped to coordinate the massive arms shipments that were supporting the Muslim Brotherhood's struggles there and throughout the Middle East.[104]

Outside of Egypt the Muslim Brotherhood was successful in creating a number of respectable front organizations and it became widely perceived as a moderate institution that had renounced violence. But inside of Egypt the Muslim Brotherhood remained committed to the overthrow of the regime and the installation of a "pure" Islamic state and they used terrorism as the means to achieve that end.

---

[103] Dreyfuss, p. 160
[104] Dreyfuss, p. 164

When Anwar Sadat became president of Egypt in 1970 he began a campaign to distance his country from Nasser's pro-Soviet policies and to realign with the West. Initially one of his most formidable opponents in this task was the Arab Socialist Unity Party. Sadat began to reconcile with the Muslim Brotherhood as a way to pressure the Arab Socialists and to solidify his regime, and he released hundreds of Muslim Brothers from prison in his first few years in office.

Throughout the history of the Muslim Brotherhood there have been six Supreme Guides. Al- Banna led until his death in 1949. He was succeeded by Hassan al-Hudaibi after a brief period of chaos in 1951. Al-Hudaibi led until his death in 1976, suffering periods of imprisonment throughout Nasser's reign. He was succeeded by Omar el-Telmisani, who died in 1987 to be succeeded by Hamid Abdul Nasr. Both Talmisani and Nasr had been thrown in prison in 1954 during Nasser's anti-Brotherhood purge. Sadat released Talmisani from prison in 1971 and Nasr in '72. The last Supreme Guide was Mustafa Mashhour, who took over in 1996 and led until his death on November 14, 2002. The present Supreme Guide is Maamoun al-Hudaibi, the eighty- three year-old son of the second Supreme Guide, Hassan al-Hudaibi. The Supreme Guide always maintains his residence and offices in Egypt, although the vast majority of members and most of its leadership is based abroad. For the most part the Supreme Guide is merely a figurehead and the clandestine operations of the Muslim Brotherhood are directed from London and Geneva.

Sadat sought to reconcile with the Islamists but he

knew they could always be a threat and he never did lift the official government ban on the Brotherhood as a political group. Even so the Brotherhood quickly emerged as a political force. Publicly the Brotherhood tried to maintain a "moderate" stance, but behind the scenes it was spawning a number of loosely connected violent extremist groups.

The *Takfir wal Hejra* was one of the most important of these groups. It was led by a former Muslim Brotherhood member, Shukri Ahmed Mustafa, and it was created in the early '70s. It was publicly exposed in 1975 by the Egyptian daily *Al Ahram* after a number of its members were arrested. In 1977 this group abducted a former minister of religion, Sheikh Mohammed Hussein al-Dhahabi, and demanded the release of sixty prisoners and 200,000 Egyptian pounds for his release. The demands were refused and the corpse of the Sheikh was turned over, followed by several targeted bombings. On July, 8, 1977, Mustafa, the leader of the group, was arrested along with a number of his followers. Mustafa and four of his ringleaders were executed on March 19, 1978, but his terrorist organization lived on.[105]

The **Organization for Islamic Liberation** was another terrorist cell created by a former Muslim Brother, a man named Dr. Saleh Siriyya. In 1974 members of this group tried to take over a military academy, capture weapons and then move on to an assembly where Sadat was speaking. The plan failed, eleven people died and Siriyya was captured and later

[105] Dietl, pp. 64-66

executed.[106]

In 1974 security forces uncovered another group, the **Islamic Liberation Party**, founded in Jordan in the '50s by Sheikh Taghiud Din Nabhani, a Muslim Brother and judge originally from Haifa. This group primarily focused activity against Israel but Sadat arrested and interrogated members of the group who lived in Egypt.[107]

The two most important Egyptian terrorist organizations that were offshoots of the Muslim Brotherhood that still exist today are the *Jamaat al-Islamiyya*, which translates as the **Islamic Group**, and **Egyptian Islamic Jihad**, also known simply as *Jihad* or *al-Jihad*. Both of them were closely involved in the assassination of President Anwar Sadat.

The *Jamaat al-Islamiyya* was created in 1971 to agitate against Sadat because of his cooperation with Libya's Qaddafi. It was headed by Muslim Brother Dr. Hilmi al-Gazzar and initially refrained from violence and focused on activism within the universities, but this was soon to change. A blind sheikh by the name of Dr. Omar Ahmed Mohammed Abdel Rahman later emerged as the leader of the organization.[108]

The other prominent group, **Islamic Jihad**, first came to light in 1977 when *Al Ahram* reported that eighty members of this fighting organization had been

---

[106] Dietl, p. 66
[107] Dietl, p. 67
[108] Dietl, p. 67

arrested. One of Islamic Jihad's members at the time was Ayman al-Zawahiri, a young upper-class Muslim related to the Azzams. His grandmother was the sister of the illustrious Abdel-Rahman Azzam mentioned previously, and his uncle was Salem Azzam of the Islamic Council of Europe. Zawahiri had first been arrested in 1966 at the age of 16 because of his Muslim Brotherhood affiliation, and his militant views continued to grow over the years.

In early 1980 Islamic Jihad was targeted again when the government arrested seventy more members. Egypt's prosecutor described the organization as a *"fanatic terrorist group,"* and said that it was *"financed from abroad and was armed with weapons, explosives and technical equipment."*[109] However, the arrests and investigation failed to prevent the ultimate terrorist attack. Dietl describes it,

"The Jihad group made the headlines once again on October 6, 1981, when a commando squad under Khaled Islambuli shot President Anwar el-Sadat. Following arduous investigations during the summer of 1982, it became known in Cairo that the Jihad group was part of the large family enterprise of the Muslim Brotherhood. When I asked, this was conceded by the Muslim Brotherhood. In the meantime, in a unanimous statement, the Jihad group 'condemned to death' Sadat's successor Mubarak. In September 1982 the three most important leaders of the Jihad group were tracked

---

[109] Dietl, p. 68, also see Zawahiri biography

down and arrested."[110]

Just two years prior to Sadat's assassination the International Committee of the Muslim Brotherhood had held a summit meeting in London. Brotherhood leaders from Egypt, Sudan, Jordan, Pakistan and Afghanistan converged, along with the head of the Saudi Arabian secret service, to discuss the recent achievements in Pakistan and Iran, and to discuss the future of Afghanistan, Syria and Egypt.[111]

In Egypt Sadat had continued to reconcile with the Muslim Brotherhood. In 1978 he allowed the Muslim Brotherhood's publication *Al Dawa* to be distributed again. In 1979 he even met with Supreme Guide Omar el-Telmisani on two occasions but nothing came of the dialogue and the Muslim Brotherhood continued its aggressive attacks on Sadat in print as well as in the mosques. Finally, just weeks before Sadat was assassinated, he had el-Telmisani arrested and a ban was placed on the distribution of *Al Dawa*.

When Sadat was gunned down Kemal al-Sananiry was the Muslim Brotherhood's most prominent representative in Egypt. He was arrested and interrogated and died in prison a few weeks later. The government lamely claimed that he had committed suicide, but his wife Amina rejected this explanation. She was the daughter of Sayed Qutb.

Also arrested, but later acquitted, was the blind sheikh,

---

[110] Dietl, p. 68
[111] Dietl, p. 61

Omar Abdul Rahman. He had encouraged the perpetrators of the assassination by ruling that the government was led by atheists and heretics. He also permitted them to steal as a means to finance their cause and even ruled that they would be allowed to have their way with the wives of government officials if they succeeded in toppling the government.[112] Years later he was implicated in the 1993 bombing of the World Trade Center, tried, convicted and sentenced to prison where he now sits. His two sons carry on the jihad as members of Al Qaeda and close followers of Osama bin Laden. They were highlighted in the cache of Al Qaeda videos that were recently publicized on CNN (see the clip *"Roots of Hatred"*). Sheikh Rahman is still the recognized spiritual leader of the Islamic Group, and its members have vowed to take revenge on America if the diabetic Sheikh dies in his American prison.

Ayman al-Zawahiri was also arrested in connection with the assassination. After spending three years in prison he was released, whereupon he soon rose to the top of Islamic Jihad, taking over in 1993, and then linking up with Osama bin Laden in Sudan. After he fled Egypt he based his operations in Geneva, Switzerland, working under the cover of the Muslim Brotherhood-controlled Islamic Center led by Said Ramadan.[113] (With whom Malcolm X had his famous correspondence just weeks prior to his assassination by Elijah Mohammed's Black Muslims.) Al-Zawahiri has emerged as the alleged "number two man" in the "Al Qaeda" organization. His

---

[112] Dietl, p. 87
[113] Bodansky, p. 101, p. 125

brother Muhammad al-Zawahiri is currently in the Balkans directing Muslim attacks against Serbia and Macedonia. Reports say that he works out of a NATO-controlled area of Kosovo.[114] These two "Azzam family" brothers have always maintained their connections with the Muslim Brotherhood, despite the fact that Ayman has publicly criticized the Brotherhood for its lack of support for the revolution in Egypt. His criticism has been a useful cover for the Brotherhood which tries to maintain its "moderate" facade.

Another important figure in the Al Qaeda organization with links back to the Sadat assassination is the brother of assassin Khaled Islambuli, who was executed on April 15, 1982. Ahmad Shawqi al-Islambuli left Egypt and appeared in Karachi, Pakistan, where he helped to set up a smuggling network. Later Islambuli worked with bin Laden in Sudan setting up a militant base in Somalia, and then he became a member of bin Laden's **World Islamic Front for Jihad Against Jews and Crusaders** in 1998.[115]

The most recent prominent terrorist offshoot of the Muslim Brotherhood is the Palestinian group **HAMAS**, which surfaced as a separate group in 1988 upon the release of its *"Islamic Covenant,"* by Sheikh Ahmed Yassin. He had been the head of the Muslim Brotherhood in Gaza for a number of years and his group can be traced back to 1978 when it was registered as an Islamic association called ***Al-Mujamma Al-Islami***. In its Islamic Covenant of 1988 the group

---

[114] Bodansky, p. 298, Balkans report
[115] Bodansky, p. 13, p. 405

plainly describes itself as the *"Palestinian branch of the Muslim Brotherhood."*[116]

Robert Dreyfuss summarizes the nature of the Muslim Brotherhood organization in the few paragraphs below. These words were written in 1980, but they are just as true today:

"The *real* Muslim Brotherhood is not the fanatical sheikh with his equally fanatical following, nor is it even the top mullahs and ayatollahs who lead entire movements of such madmen; Khomeini, Qaddafi, General Zia are exquisitely fashioned puppets. The real Muslim Brothers are those whose hands are never dirtied with the business of killing and burning.

They are the secretive bankers and financiers who stand behind the curtain, the members of the old Arab, Turkish, or Persian families whose genealogy places them in the oligarchical elite, with smooth business and intelligence associations to the European black nobility and, especially, to the British oligarchy. And the Muslim Brotherhood is money. Together, the Brotherhood probably controls several tens of billions of dollars in immediate liquid assets, and controls billions more in day-to-day business operations in everything from oil trade and banking to drug-running, illegal arms merchandising, and gold and diamond smuggling. By allying with the Muslim

---

[116] Hamas background & profile:
http://www.fas.org/irp/world/para/docs/970824.htm

Brotherhood, the Anglo-Americans are not merely buying into a terrorists-for-hire racket; they are partners in a powerful and worldwide financial empire that extends from numbered Swiss bank accounts to offshore havens in Dubai, Kuwait and Hong Kong."[117]

Hopefully the reader is beginning to understand how small the radical Islamist movement really is, how closely inter-connected it is, and how it all seems to tie back into the Muslim Brotherhood. The picture gets even clearer when the career of Osama bin Laden is closely inspected.

---

[117] Dreyfuss, pp. 164-165

IV.   Osama bin Laden: The Early Years

Osama was born around 1957, the seventeenth son of the Yemenite construction magnate Sheikh Mohammed bin Oud bin Laden. Over the years Mohammed had established himself as a trusted friend of King Abdul Aziz and then King Feisal of Saudi Arabia, and his construction firm was hired to refurbish the holy sites in Mecca and Medina, including Mecca's Grand Mosque. He also received a contract to refurbish the Al-Aqsa Mosque in Jerusalem in 1969.

At the time of Mohammed bin Laden's death in 1972 his family had grown to become perhaps the richest non-royal family in Saudi Arabia, and his estate was handed over to his fifty-four children. His son Salem emerged as the head of the firm, and then Bakr, with Abdelaziz, Ali, Yeslam and Yahya emerged also playing leading roles in directing the bin Laden empire. These heirs have always enjoyed a close relationship with the Saudi royal family and are responsible for training many of the younger Saudi princes in the intricacies of global finance and industry. Mohammed bin Fahd and Saud bin Nayef are two of the princes who owe their current status as global tycoons to the bin Laden brothers.[118] The Saudi royal family has always been close with the top levels of the bin Laden family, but the same cannot be said about some of the younger sons of Mohammed bin Laden.

---

[118] *In the Name of Osama Bin Laden,* Roland Jacquard, 2001, pp.12-13

On November 20, 1979, Mecca's Grand Mosque was taken over by several hundred militants. The Imam was murdered and in the chaos thousands of worshipers were trampled to death. The militants took hundreds of hostages and holed up in the vast cellars under the mosque. Saudi forces reacted quickly and staged a counter-attack against the rebels inside but they were easily repulsed by the well-armed and well-fortified militants. For days the rebels fought off the government forces, destroying tanks and even a helicopter that flew in too close, crashing into a minaret. Finally King Khalid turned to the French government and French special forces arrived with chemical weapons to smoke out the rebels. The Grand Mosque was finally liberated on December 4. For two weeks the holiest shrine of Islam had been taken over by radical fundamentalists. The end result was hundreds of government soldiers and over a hundred rebels dead, with most of the hostages dead as well. On January 9 sixty-three of the captured rebels were paraded into the main squares of several Arabian cities and publicly beheaded. Hundreds more were arrested and interrogated in the ensuing investigation.[119]

Among those arrested was Mahrous bin Laden, son of Sheikh Mohammed bin Laden and brother of Osama. In his biography of Osama bin Laden Jacquard writes:

"The terrorists had established contact with Mahrous several years earlier, when he was a student in London and when he counted among his friends the son of a Southern Yemeni dignitary,

---

[119] Dietl, pp. 211-227

the leader of a very active fundamentalist group. Following this university connection, Mahrous bin Laden became involved with a group of Syrian Muslim Brotherhood activists exiled to Saudi Arabia. The Saudi secret service investigation ultimately declared Mahrous innocent. The investigation stated that by exploiting networks of the young Mahrous's former friendships, the terrorists had gained access to the bin Laden group's trucks to organize their attack without the young man's knowledge."[120] p.13-14

The Bin Laden firm was responsible for the Grand Mosque's renovations and so its trucks were allowed to come and go freely without being searched. The terrorists had used these trucks to help them smuggle in weapons that were then stashed inside the mosque prior to the takeover.

Mahrous was declared innocent of being involved in this intrigue but his honor was tainted forever and he knew he could never rise to the level of achievement reached by his older brothers. Had he been the member of any other family it is likely that he would have been executed, if only for simply having relations with some of the fundamentalists linked to the terrorists. In the end it was the bin Laden family that saved the day, because they provided the blueprints of the mosque that helped to plan the final successful attacks against the rebels. In the end the bin Laden family emerged from the whole affair pretty much unscathed, with their integrity and their close relationship with the House of

---

[120] Jacquard, pp.13-14

Saud intact.[121]

Osama bin Laden, as one of the youngest sons of the bin Laden family, grew up feeling somewhat of an outsider and like his brother Mahrous he turned to fundamentalist Islam. Biographer Adam Robinson states that the young Osama lived a very indulgent and secular lifestyle during his teenage years, especially while he attended high school in Beirut from 1973 to 1975. Others, such as Roland Jacquard argue that this was not the case. Whatever the truth of his younger days, it is clear that Osama wholeheartedly embraced Islam during the time that he attended King Abdul Aziz University in Jeddah. He enrolled there in 1976 and in 1977 he undertook the two-week long holy Muslim pilgrimage to Mecca, the *Hajj*. Robinson writes that after this experience Osama began to grow his beard long and his sincerity towards Islam became apparent. What Robinson does not divulge is that Osama's exposure to the Muslim Brotherhood at this time brought about his conversion.

Mohammed Qutb, the brother of Sayed Qutb the "chief ideologist" of the Muslim Brotherhood who was executed in 1966, emigrated to Saudi Arabia as a result of Nasser's crackdown on the Brotherhood. In the 1960s he was given several different official positions within Saudi universities to teach and to carry out the mission of the Muslim Brotherhood. While in Saudi Arabia Mohammed Qutb conceived of the organization now known as the **World Assembly of Muslim Youth**, and it was made a reality in 1972 thanks to large

[121] Jacquard, pp.13-14

donations from the bin Laden family. Osama's brother Omar was at one time its executive director, and another brother, Abdullah, also served as a director.[122] WAMY was being investigated as a source of terrorist funding until the Bush administration halted the FBI's investigation at the beginning of his term in 2001.

WAMY's perspective on Islam is the familiar Muslim Brotherhood perspective that the Globalists like so much, that Islam is threatened by the West and that it must remain wary of science and technology and return to its primitive roots. WAMY's headquarters today are in Riyadh, with major offices in Falls Church, Virginia and London, England. According to reporter Greg Palast there are over twenty WAMY-aligned organizations also based in Britain.[123]

While attending King Abdul Aziz University in Jeddah Osama bin Laden became close to Mohammed Qutb and he was initiated into the Muslim Brotherhood. Malise Ruthven, author of Islam In the World and former editor with the BBC Arabic Service, even remarks that Qutb was Osama's "*mentor*" during this period.[124]

Another important figure in Osama's university life was a professor by the name of Sheikh Abdullah Yussuf Azzam. Unrelated to the Egyptian Azzams, he was a Palestinian-born teacher of religion who was an active

---

[122] Qutb- *personal correspondence with the Italian Muslim Association*, *Omar and Abdullah* - article
[123] *The Guardian* article by Greg Palast
[124] *The Guardian* article by Malise Ruthven

member of the Muslim Brotherhood in the West Bank. Later he pursued an education in Jordan and Damascus before receiving his doctorate in Islamic jurisprudence from Cairo's *Al Azhar* University in 1973. While in Cairo he met the family of Sayed Qutb and was "*drawn into the ranks of the Egyptian militant Islamists.*"[125] Shortly after this he moved to Saudi Arabia after being invited to teach at King Abdul Aziz University, where he linked up with Mohammed Qutb. Osama attended Azzam's classes and was caught up into his militant ideology. Azzam's famous motto was,

"Jihad and the rifle alone: no negotiations, no conferences, and no dialogues."[126]

In 1979 Dr. Azzam left Saudi Arabia and was one of the first Arabs to join the Afghan jihad. He was the lead Saudi/Palestinian representative of the Muslim Brotherhood. The 22-year old Osama bin Laden followed soon after and together they established the *Maktab al-Khidamat*, MAK, or Mujahideen Services Bureau based in Peshawar, Afghanistan. Their organization linked up with Pakistan's Muslim Brotherhood organization, the *Jamaat-e Islami*. The MAK worked to recruit fighters to join the jihad and by the late 1980s there were branches of the MAK, known also as the Al Kifah Organization, in fifty countries around the world. The Muslim Brotherhood network combined with bin Laden family money to make the MAK a tremendous success.

---

[125] *Bin Laden: The Man Who Declared War on America*, Yossef Bodansky, 1999 p. 11
[126] Bodansky, p. 11

Militants from around the globe poured into Afghanistan, but Azzam and bin Laden recognized that many of the prospective mujahedin lacked the necessary training and supplies for the Afghan campaign. To remedy this they established *Masadat Al-Ansar* in Peshawar as a central base, training compound and storehouse to serve the Arabs coming in to fight.[127] Bodansky p. 12 This was *Al Qaeda* (the base) for the thousands streaming in to fight the jihad. Dr. Saad al-Fagih was one of the many Saudis who passed through the Peshawar base, and he explained in a PBS interview how Al Qaeda came to be and how it was never meant to refer to bin Laden's terrorist organization:

"Well, I [really] laugh when I hear the FBI talking about Al Qaeda as an organization of bin Laden... [It's really a] very simple story. If bin Laden is to receive Arabs from Saudi Arabia and from Kuwait-- from other regions--he is [to] receive them in the guest house in Peshawar. They used to go to the battle field and come back, without documentation... There [was] no documentation of who has arrived. Who has left. How long he stayed. There's only [a nice general reception]. And you go there. And you join in the battle field... Now, he was embarrassed by many families when they called him and ask what happened to our son. He doesn't know.
`Cause there's no record. There's no documentation. Now he asked some of his colleagues to start documenting the movement of every Arab coming under his umbrella... It is

[127] Bodansky, p. 12

recorded that [they] arrived in this date and stayed in this house... Many of them had come only for two weeks, three weeks and then disappeared. That record, that documentation was called the record of Al Qaeda. So that was Al Qaeda. There's nothing sinister about Al Qaeda. It's not like an organization... I don't think he used any name for his underground group. If you want to name it, you can name it 'bin Laden group.' But if they are using the term Al Qaeda ... Al Qaeda is just a record for the people who came to Peshawar and moved from there back and forth to the guest house. And moved back to their country."[128]

Bin Laden's years fighting the Afghan war were mostly spent in Pakistan and his job was primarily that of a fundraiser and an organizer, although many times he would travel into Afghanistan with his mentor Sheikh Azzam, known as the 'Emir of Jihad,' who would give fiery speeches to raise the morale of the mujahedin warriors. In Afghanistan bin Laden's resources as a contractor were also used and he brought in heavy equipment on a number of occasions to help fortify mujahedin strongholds and to refurbish supply roads. The debate is still unsettled as to whether or not bin Laden or Azzam were ever involved in any actual front-line fighting, but both have been mythologized as active and courageous warriors.

During bin Laden's Afghan years the MAK developed close relations with Pashtun warlord and Muslim Brother Gulbuddin Hekmatyar. Azzam and Hekmatyar

---

128 Al-Faqih interview

both held anti-American views, but Hekmatyar's were more pronounced, even though it is estimated that his group, the **Hezb-e-Islami**, received up to 40% of the American aid channeled to the mujahedin through the CIA and the ISI.[129] During the 1980's Azzam also traveled throughout the USA meeting American Muslim groups, raising funds and recruiting fighters for the jihad. He set up major Al Kifah centers in Atlanta, Boston, Chicago, Brooklyn, Jersey City, Pittsburgh, and Tucson, and smaller Al Kifah branches in thirty other American cities.[130] In this way the militant Muslim Brotherhood message was dispersed throughout the United States and recruits were brought into the jihad.

According to respected Pakistani journalist Ahmed Rashid the Afghan war escalated in 1986 when the CIA made three strategic decisions.[131] First, to provide the mujahedin with American made Stinger missiles. At the height of the war it is estimated that the mujahedin averaged 1.5 kills per day of Soviet and communist Afghan aircraft. The second decision was one promoted by British Intelligence and the ISI to launch guerilla attacks into Soviet territory in Tajikistan and Uzbekistan. Predictably, the operation was handed over to Hekmatyar's forces, who managed to achieve a symbolic success, to which the Soviets responded by firebombing all nearby villages. The CIA immediately stopped this action as counter-productive. Thirdly, the CIA began to endorse the Arab initiative of recruiting

---

[129] Jacquard, p. 57
[130] Al Kifah article
[131] *Islam in Central Asia: Afghanistan and Pakistan*, Ahmed Rashid, pp. 213-214

jihad warriors around the world. Rashid describes how this recruiting drive was run,

"Pakistan had issued standing instructions to all its embassies abroad to give visas, with no questions asked, to anyone wanting to come and fight with the *mujahidin*. In the Middle East the Ikhwan ul Muslimeen (Muslim Brotherhood), the Saudi-based World Muslim League, and the Palestinian Islamic radicals organized recruits and put them in contact with the ISI. The ISI and Pakistan's Jamaat-e-Islami Party set up reception committees to welcome, house, and train the foreign militants. Then the two encouraged militants to join the *mujahidin* groups, usually the Hizbe Islami. Much of the funding for this enterprise came directly from Saudi Intelligence, which was partly channeled through the Saudi radical Osama bin Laden, who was then based in Peshawar. At the time, French scholar Oliver Roy described the enterprise as 'a joint venture between the Saudis, the Muslim Brotherhood, and the Jamaat-e-Islami, put together by the ISI.'"[132]

These three decisions escalated the war in Afghanistan and made it clear to Mikhail Gorbachev that his nation was fighting a battle that it could never win. On April 14, 1988 the Geneva Accords were signed mandating a Soviet withdrawal from Afghanistan. By early 1989 the Soviet Army was out of Afghanistan, but a staunchly communist and well-armed Afghan regime was still ruling from Kabul.

---

[132] Rashid, p. 214

American aid to the mujahedin ended almost precisely at the moment the Geneva Accords were signed. The Soviets were leaving and so the West congratulated itself on achieving a victory. For the United States the war was over and the CIA did not want to participate in creating an Islamist regime in Afghanistan that would undoubtedly be anti-American. As a result Hekmatyar, Azzam, bin Laden and the Islamist warlords were left feeling betrayed and used.

The mujahedin also received a major setback on August 17, 1988, when General Muhammed Zia ul-Haq, Pakistan's ruling dictator and mentor of the mujahedin, died when his C-130 aircraft crashed minutes after taking off from Bahawalpur airport. Also killed were a number of generals and the American ambassador. In November of 1988, Benazir Bhutto, the daughter of Zulfikar Bhutto who had been executed by General Zia, was elected Prime Minister. She began to introduce policies that threatened the fundamentalists and the warlords, including legislation that cracked down on drug smuggling.

In March of 1989 the mujahedin were convinced by Saudi and ISI advisors to launch a full-scale assault on the communist-held city of Jalalabad. It was argued that the fall of Jalalabad would lead to a quick route of President Najibullah's forces and that Afghanistan could then be quickly liberated. The assault turned into one of the biggest disasters for the mujahedin because Jalalabad was well-defended and protected by a veteran army that included a significant artillery contingent. The mujahedin were slaughtered by the thousands.

Back in Peshawar bin Laden and Azzam reacted in fury. They began to issue statements from their press offices accusing Pakistan and Saudi Arabia of being part of a treacherous American plot. This was perhaps the first public notice of bin Laden's growing resentment towards the decidedly pro-American Saudi regime of his homeland.[133]

A greater blow struck bin Laden when his friend and father-figure Sheikh Abdullah Azzam was assassinated several months later. Notice the mythology that surrounds the passing of this man as related on a Muslim web site:

"On Friday the 24th of November 1989 in Peshawar, Pakistan, he was assassinated along with his two sons Mohammed and Ibrahim, by 20kg of TNT activated by remote control while he was driving to Friday (Jumma) prayer. His car was blown apart into fragments in the middle of a busy street. The blast was so intensive that fragments from the bodies of his sons were found up to a hundred meters from the carnage. One of his son's legs was also found suspended from an overhead telephone line. Nevertheless, Allah be glorified, the Sheikh was found perfectly intact, except for an internal haemorrhage, which caused his death. Many a people present will confirm to the smell of musk that emanated from his body."[134]

In his early days Sheikh Azzam had helped to create the

---

[133] *Bin Laden: Behind the Mask of the Terrorist*, Adam Robinson, 2001, p. 112
[134] Abdullah Azzam biography

Palestinian organization now known as HAMAS. Today the military wing of HAMAS on the West Bank is officially known as the **Abdullah Azzam Brigades**.[135] In London the **Azzam Organization** was founded in his name and its affiliate Azzam Publications (www.azzam.com) describes itself as "*an independent media organization providing authentic news and information about Jihad and the Foreign Mujahideen everywhere.*" The website was shut down after September 11, 2001.[136]

At the end of 1989 Osama bin Laden returned to Saudi Arabia. He was welcomed as a celebrity and a hero, but he remained bitter about the political infighting that was consuming Afghanistan and cynical of the ruling House of Saud. He turned back to his family and he briefly took up a job within the Bin Laden Firm working in road construction. He was 32, and almost a ten-year veteran of the Afghan war, but his jihad days were just beginning. The Muslim Brotherhood had further plans for him.

---

[135] Abdullah Azzam article
[136] Radical Islam in the UK, report

V.   Bin Laden In Exile

On August 2, 1990, Iraq invaded Kuwait and bin Laden's easy lifestyle received a jolt. Suddenly there was a new threat to be dealt with and a new mission for him to embrace. On the day of the invasion bin Laden flew from his home in Jeddah by private jet to the capital of Riyadh. He went directly to the offices of King Fahd and was met by Prince Sultan. He offered the prince a handwritten ten-page memorandum in which he offered to raise an army of 10,000 battle- hardened mujahedin veterans to complement the Saudi Arabian army, to liberate Kuwait and drive out Saddam Hussein's army. Biographer Adam Robinson describes the situation:

"Family members recall that for several days after making the offer Osama remained glued to his mobile telephone, expecting a reply from King Fahd. He called the monarch's office repeatedly, contacted several of King Fahd's aides to repeat the offer, sent several faxes and dispatched members of his office staff to the king's office with copies of his letters. Meanwhile he worked day and night in his office marshalling his forces, mobilising them in preparation for action, confident that they would be the key to success in the war that lay ahead. But then, on August 7, came the snub that has consumed and angered him until this day."[137]

---

[137] *Bin Laden: Behind the Mask of the Terrorist*, Adam Robinson, 2001, p. 130

On that day it was announced that King Fahd had agreed to allow a coalition of American-led forces to occupy Saudi Arabian territory to protect his regime and to prepare to liberate Kuwait. The Bush Administration had panicked King Fahd with *reports* of satellite photos showing Hussein's forces massing on the border preparing for a Saudi invasion. The reports were entirely bogus, the satellite photos did not exist and the threat was a complete fabrication. Iraq had no intention of invading Saudi Arabia, as they attempted to make clear through diplomatic channels and the international media. Nevertheless King Fahd was intimidated into believing that his regime was in danger and he allowed the occupation and troop buildup for Desert Storm.[138]

Osama bin Laden, along with the Islamic leadership within Saudi Arabia and around the world, considered this foreign occupation of holy Muslim lands to be an abomination. Bodansky describes the problem faced by King Fahd:

"In early August 1990 King Fahd asked the *ulema* - the country's senior religious leaders- to endorse the deployment of U.S. forces. 'All the senior ulema were categorically against the idea,' a Saudi official said in a study by exiled Saudi scholar Nawaf Obaid. 'It was only after long discussions with the King that Grand Mufti Sheikh Abdul-Aziz Bin Baz reluctantly gave his endorsement to the idea on condition that solid proof be presented as to the [Iraqi] threat.' ...Word of this conflict between the

Saudi Court and the ulema spread like wildfire throughout the Islamist circles of Saudi Arabia."[139]

Bin Laden had this to say about King Fahd in a 1998 interview:

"Any government that sells its peoples' interests and betrays its people and takes action that remove it from the Muslim nation will not succeed. We predict that the Riyadh leader and those with him that stood with the Jews and Christians with American identities or other, will disintegrate. They have left the Muslim nation. We predict that like the Iran royal family, the Shah, they will disperse and disappear. After Allah gave them property on the most sacred land and gave them wealth that is unheard of before from oil, still they sinned and did not value Allah's gift. We predict destruction and dispersal..."[140]

Operation Desert Storm ended on February 28, 1991, but as the foreign occupation continued, so did bin Laden's outspoken criticism of the Saudi regime. He gave speeches at meetings and at mosques and as a result he began to be closely monitored by the Saudi secret police. Bin Laden began to receive threats and Robinson writes of relatives that recall that on one occasion he was even cornered and beaten up by a group of "youths" (allegedly Saudi secret service agents) for criticizing the government.[141] Bin Laden began to

[139] Bodansky, p. 130
[140] Robinson, p. 131
[141] Robinson, p. 132

realize that he was not welcome in his home country and that he would be better able to pursue his goals outside of Saudi Arabia. In April of 1991 he was able to leave under the pretext of signing a business deal in Pakistan. He had no intention of returning.

Bin Laden spent about eight months in Pakistan and Afghanistan, but even there he did not feel completely free. The Pakistan government was not especially friendly to Islamists at this time and bin Laden often heard rumors that Saudi Intelligence was working with the ISI to arrest him and bring him back to Saudi Arabia. His close relationship with Gulbuddin Hekmatyar was a problem as well, because Hekmatyar had angered the Saudis through his strong support for Saddam Hussein during Desert Storm. Throughout the Middle East the Islamists were feeling a backlash. Afghanistan was in the midst of a civil war, Saudi Arabia and Pakistan were cracking down, Iran was Shi'ite and unwelcome towards Sunnis, and Egypt was cracking down as well. As a result many of the most fanatical Islamists fled to London, where they were always accepted, or to the newly established Islamic Republic of Sudan, to which bin Laden was invited.

Sudan had become an official bastion of Islamic Fundamentalism starting on June 30, 1989, when General Omar Hassan al-Bashir took over in a military coup. In August, just a few months later, Sudan's role was confirmed at a London meeting of the International Muslim Brotherhood. The Sudanese delegate was a man by the name of Hassan al-Turabi, who would emerge as the real power behind the throne in Sudan, and a mentor to Osama bin Laden.

Hassan al-Turabi was born in 1932, educated in English-language schools in Sudan and indoctrinated into Islam by his father. He graduated the British-run Gordon College in Khartoum in 1955 with a law degree, and sometime during this time he joined the Muslim Brotherhood. After Gordon College he received a scholarship to attend the University of London, where he received his masters degree in law. Turabi then attended the Sorbonne University in France receiving his doctorate in 1964. Back in Sudan he emerged as the intellectual leader and spokesman of the Islamist movement and the leader of the Sudanese branch of the Muslim Brotherhood. He became known as the Black Pope of Africa.[142]

At the Muslim Brotherhood meeting in London in 1989 it was decided that Sudan would be a new base for the Islamist movement, and a Muslim Brotherhood leadership council of nineteen members was subsequently established in Khartoum under Turabi. This council helped to organize the Islamist movement in the chaotic aftermath of the Afghan-Soviet war and in April 1991 a conference called the "Islamic Arab People's Conference" was held in Khartoum. This was a congress of Islamist and terrorist groups from around the world and it helped to establish the **Popular International Organization**. The PIO then established another council in Khartoum of fifty members, one each from the fifty countries around the world that were engaged in an Islamic struggle.[143]

---

[142] Bodansky, p. 32
[143] Bodansky, p. 36

The International Muslim Brotherhood does more than just create councils and more councils. The IMB also controls the "International Legion of Islam" or "Islamic Legion." It emerged during the 1980s and was based primarily in Pakistan and Afghanistan, and also in Tehran, (earlier we covered the role the Muslim Brotherhood played in evicting the Shah and setting up the hardline Shi'ite regime of the Ayatollah Khomeini). During the 1990's the Islamic Legion would work most effectively out of Khartoum. The Islamic Legion is simply an unofficial loose- knit military organization that helps to coordinate the global jihad. Yossef Bodansky, the director of the Congressional Task Force on Terrorism and Unconventional Warfare and author of the bin Laden biography sited often in this study, refers to the Islamic Legion as the **Armed Islamic Movement** or **AIM**.

The Islamist movement suffered a huge blow on July 5, 1991 when the **Bank of Credit and Commerce International** was finally shut down by the Bank of England. As related in Part One, this bank was an important conduit of drug profits and money laundering that also served as a broker for illegal arms deals. It had been an important component of the global Islamist movement's financial network and now it had been dissolved. Before the movement could rise to its potential its leaders knew that a new financial network had to be set up. This may be one of the reasons for inviting bin Laden to Sudan, because bin Laden was married to the sister of Khalid bin Mahfouz. In the book *"Forbidden Truth: U.S.-Taliban Secret Oil Diplomacy and the Failed Hunt for Bin Laden,"* the French authors describe Mahfouz:

"Khalid bin Mahfouz was a key figure in the Bank of Credit and Commerce International, or BCCI, affair. Between 1986 and 1990, he was a top executive there, holding the position of operational director. His family held a 20 percent share in the bank at the time. He was charged in the United States in 1992 with tax fraud in the bank's collapse. In 1995, held jointly liable in the BCCI's collapse, he agreed to a $245 million settlement to pay the bank's creditors, allowing them to indemnify a portion of the bank's clients. The specific charges against the bank were embezzlement and violation of American, Luxembourg and British banking laws.

After dominating the financial news throughout the 1990s the BCCI is now at the center of the financial network put in place by Osama bin Laden's main supporters."[144]

In 1999 the French Parliament commissioned an intense and thorough investigation of global money-laundering. After publishing reports on Liechtenstein, Monaco and Switzerland it produced, on October 10, 2001, the conclusions of its investigations into the banking system of Great Britain: **"The City of London, Gibraltar and the Crown Dependencies: Offshore Centers and Havens for Dirty Money."**

Attached to the 400-page report was a 70-page addendum entitled **"The Economic Environment of**

---

[144] *Forbidden Truth,* Jean-Charles Brisard and Guillaume Dasquie, 2002, p. 117

Osama bin Laden" that focused specifically on the London-based financial network associated with Osama bin Laden. The report concludes that up to forty British banks, companies and individuals were associated with bin Laden's network, including organizations in London, Oxford, Cheltenham, Cambridge and Leeds. In introducing the report French Member of Parliament Arnaud Montebourg said, *"Tony Blair, and his government, preaches around the world against terrorism. He would be well advised to preach to his own bankers and oblige them to go after dirty money... Even the Swiss co-operate more than the English."*[145]

French investigator Jean-Charles Brisard (who I believe worked on the report) offers this conclusion in his book *Forbidden Truth*:

"The financial network surrounding Osama bin Laden and his investments is similar in structure to the fraudulent network put in place in the 1980s by the BCCI. They even share some of the same personalities (former BCCI executives and directors, oil and arms dealers, Saudi investors) and, sometimes, the same companies (NCB, Attock oil, BAII).

The study points out the fact that BCCI financing networks have survived, even though Osama bin Laden receives parallel support from political or terrorist movements from the Islamist sphere of influence.
The convergence of financial interests and terrorist

---

[145] *"UK is money launderers' paradise,"* BBC News article

**activities, especially Great Britain and Sudan, does
not seem to have been an obstacle to each group's
desired objectives.
A terrorist network backed by a vast financing
system is the trademark of Osama bin Laden's
operations."**[146]

And now I am going to introduce a thesis that we will
return to often throughout the rest of this study. It is
simply this, that Osama bin Laden is not the head of
this covert, shadowy financial network that has surfaced
occasionally as a source of funding for bin Laden's
terrorist activities. Osama bin Laden is not, nor has he
ever been, the leader of the international Islamist
movement which is directed by the International
Muslim Brotherhood. Osama bin Laden has been used
effectively as a *figurehead* for the Brotherhood's
militant branch to take responsibility for its atrocities,
but he is not the *mastermind* of the entire operation,
or even of the operations which he is asked to direct or
take responsibility for.

By the same token the Muslim Brotherhood is being
used as a tool by the British-based Globalists whose
main objective is to overthrow the established world
order and create a new one-world system of global
governance. But we will get to this secondary and more
sensational thesis later.

The International Muslim Brotherhood had used the
BCCI to finance its activities up until its closure in July
of 1991. When this happened, which was after all of the

---

[146] Brisard and Dasquie, pp. 184-185

important high-level Islamist meetings had already taken place in Sudan, Osama bin Laden was brought in to help organize the rebuilding of the network in December of 1991. Bin Laden had established a reputation as an excellent organizer during his years with the MAK in Peshawar and so he was the perfect man for the job, and his close relationship with his brother-in-law Khalid bin Mahfouz was an added benefit. Mahfouz knew the British banking establishment like the back of his hand and he knew exactly which British banks and bankers could be trusted to help rebuild the covert quasi-legal network. Adam Robinson writes about the resurrection of this network, which owed a great debt to the organizer bin Laden,

"Within months, Osama unveiled before an astonished al-Turabi what he called 'the Brotherhood Group' [author- yes, the 'Brotherhood Group']. **This was a network of 134 Arab businessmen whose combined commercial empire extended around the globe and back many times. They maintained bank accounts in virtually every country and, collectively, routinely shifted billions of dollars around as part of their legitimate businesses. It was a perfect front. The Brotherhood Group came to be utilised by terror groups all around the world. Osama was the toast of his industry."**[147]

Bin Laden also helped to invigorate Sudan's own failing banking industry when he invested $50 million to

---

[147] Robinson, p. 139 also see Bodansky, p. 43

capitalize the El Shamal Islamic Bank of Khartoum. This was bin Laden's bank, owned in partnership with Sudan's **National Islamic Front**, which is simply the Sudanese branch of the International Muslim Brotherhood.

After helping to reestablish the Muslim Brotherhood's financial network bin Laden was kept busy in Sudan on projects related to his profession as a contractor. A company was set up jointly controlled by bin Laden, the Sudanese military and Sudan's National Islamic Front called **Al-Hijra for Construction and Development Ltd.** Major projects were tackled including the development of Port Sudan on the Red Sea, an airport at Port Sudan and a four lane highway over the 650 miles from the Port to Khartoum. Al-Hijra also undertook a project to widen the Blue Nile and to build the Rosaires Dam. Work was also done to improve the rail lines, several smaller airports were built, and roads were paved throughout the country.[148]

While bin Laden was being kept busy building Sudan's infrastructure, the International Muslim Brotherhood (IMB) was preparing to confront the United States Military in Somalia. While the intent to insert American forces into Somalia for "humanitarian purposes" was not publicized until late 1992, the IMB seemed to anticipate American intervention almost from the time that the Somalian government fell in January of 1992. It's almost as if the U.S. Military's mission to Somalia was pre-arranged to confront the Islamists, and to fail.

---

[148] Bodansky, p. 46, Robinson, pp. 139-140

As was noted earlier, Sudan announced its intention to become a militant base for the IMB at the London meeting of 1989. After that, organizations such as the one run by Abu Nidal, HAMAS, and Iran/Lebanon's Hezbollah set up offices in Khartoum. Soon after training camps were opened and bin Laden was invited in. Also in late 1991 Iran and Sudan began to form a strategic friendship. This cooperation between militant Shi'ite and Sunni Fundamentalism immediately caught the attention of the regimes in Egypt and Saudi Arabia and it was understood that Sudan was emerging as a threat.

Hassan al-Turabi also made the diplomatic rounds in the West. According to bin Laden biographer Roland Jacquard, Turabi visited London in 1992 and was a guest at the **Royal Institute of International Affairs**. This is the headquarters of the British Globalists and the parent organization of America's **Council on Foreign Relations**. After this visit he also took a trip to the United States, where he was given an official reception in Washington.[149] Back in Sudan Turabi established links with Somalian warlord Muhammad Farah Aidid. Bodansky explains:

"The Somalian terrorists were provided with equipment and weapons for the militias they would train and lead. Some of these militias operated within the ranks of the main Somalian parties, while others were completely independent, answering only to Khartoum... Tehran, which controlled and sponsored these Somalian terrorists

---

[149] Jacquard, p. 32

via Sudan, planned on using them against the U.S. forces the same way the HizbAllah had been used by Syria and Iran against the U.S. peacekeepers in Beirut in the early 1980s."[150]

In late 1992 the IMB also called upon Sheikh Tariq al-Fadli to return to Yemen from his comfortable exile in London to organize a terrorist cell to strike the American forces that would soon be passing through on their way to Somalia. Bin Laden had known al-Fadli from the Afghan campaign, and bin Laden was instrumental in linking the sheikh up with the thousands of Yemeni "Afghans" that had returned home. Al-Fadli was inserted into Yemen in "mid-November" according to Bodansky, while the intention to commit American forces to Somalia was not revealed by the Clinton Administration until November 28.[151]

American forces landed on the beaches of Somalia on December 9, 1992, as captured ridiculously by the floodlights of the waiting horde of international media. From the beginning the world, the majority of American citizens, and especially American servicemen and women, wondered what in the hell the US Military was doing trying to impose order upon the chaotic and unappreciative Islamic country of Somalia.

Initially the operation appeared to be a success, and the humanitarian aid was allowed to pass through, but the Islamists were simply biding their time waiting to strike. The first attack took place in Yemen, on December 29,

---

[150] Bodansky, p. 43
[151] Bodansky, p. 71

1992. Al-Fadli's newly-organized Yemeni Islamic Jihad detonated bombs in the Aden Hotel and Golden Moor Hotel, killing three and wounding five. One of the bombs barely missed hitting a contingent of 100 American marines on their way to Somalia. Another team armed with RPGs failed as well, caught near the fences of an airport where U.S. Air Force transport planes were parked nearby. Al-Fadli and a few of his followers surrendered on January 8, 1993. The rest of the Yemeni "Afghans" were airlifted to Somalia by Osama bin Laden in a covert operation in the middle of 1993. Bin Laden later boasted in an interview that this operation cost him $3 million of *his own money*.[152]

On June 5, 1993, back in Mogadishu General Aidid's forces ambushed and killed a Pakistani detachment of UN forces, killing twenty-three blue-helmeted soldiers. Aidid left Somalia and turned up later in June in Khartoum to appear at a top-level Islamist meeting. Turabi, bin Laden, a number of Iranian agents, and the head of Egyptian Islamic Jihad, Ayman al-Zawahiri, also attended. The meeting was focused on evicting the United States and the UN from Somalia. Bodansky writes that the operation was headed by Turabi, with Zawahiri, along with several other Arab "Afghans" serving under him as the military commanders. Bin Laden, like always, was responsible for the logistical support. In the fall of 1993 Zawahiri entered Somalia where he coordinated operations with Aidid's senior commanders.[153]

[152] Bodansky, p. 74
[153] Bodansky, pp. 76-78

The resistance to Operation Restore Hope peaked on October 3, 1993, with the events that have been memorably re-enacted in the Hollywood movie **"Blackhawk Down."** On this day Aidid's forces managed to shoot down two Blackhawk helicopters, wound seventy-eight American soldiers, kill eighteen and capture another. Up to a thousand Somali fighters and civilians were killed in the carnage. After this incident it became apparent to the Clinton Administration that the Somali operation needed to come to an end. By March of 1994 almost all of the American forces had pulled out, leaving the Islamists in control.

Bin Laden considered this another great victory for Islam. First the Soviets had been beaten and expelled from Afghanistan, and now the United States had been beaten and expelled from Somalia. Two superpowers had been defeated by the strength of Islam. Robinson relates the following interview of bin Laden,

"The so-called superpowers vanished into thin air. We think that the United States is very much weaker than Russia. Based on the reports we received from our brothers who participated in jihad in Somalia, we learned that they saw the weakness, frailty, and cowardice of US troops. Only 80 US troops were killed. Nonetheless, they fled in the heart of darkness, frustrated, after they had caused great commotion about the new world order..."[154]

---

[154] Robinson, p. 153

VI.   World Trade Center 1993

Under Hassan al-Turabi Sudan had achieved a great
victory for the Muslim Brotherhood by evicting the
United States from Somalia. But even prior to the
Somalia engagement the Muslim Brotherhood was
involved in a major strike at the heart of the United
States. On February 26, 1993 the World Trade Center
bombing occurred in which six people were killed and
up to a thousand more were wounded, with the cost of
damages over $250 million. The intention of the
bomber, Ramzi Youssef, was to topple one tower onto
the other, and at the same time disperse a cloud of
cyanide gas over New York City. Fortunately the
explosion in the underground parking structure was not
enough to topple the tower, but it was enough to burn
up the cyanide gas making it ineffective.

The mainstream media focused on the blind sheikh
Omar Abdul Rahman, who was arrested, tried and
convicted for being involved in the conspiracy. He was
the leader of the *Jamaat al- Islamiyya* (the **Islamic
Group**), who had been imprisoned in Egypt for his
moral support of the murderers of Anwar Sadat. When
he was released in 1985 he made his way to Pakistan
where he linked up with Gulbuddin Hekmatyar and
Abdullah Azzam. He became a very famous cleric
within Islamist circles, well known for his fearless
militant preaching, and for his hatred of President
Mubarak of Egypt. Throughout the late '80s he
constantly traveled preaching in Islamic centers
throughout Saudi Arabia and even in Britain, Germany
and the United States, with the blessing of the CIA. He
also met several times with Hassan al-Turabi in

Khartoum and London.[155]

In May of 1990 he acquired a visa from the American consulate in Khartoum, from a CIA agent posing as an official, despite the fact that his name was on a State Department list of terrorist suspects. Rahman settled in New Jersey where he began to preach the same militant message that he had always preached. In November of 1990 the State Department revoked Sheikh Rahman's visa and advised the INS to be on the lookout for him. Five months later the INS, instead of deporting him, issued Rahman a green card.[156]

Sheikh Rahman's move to the United States was sponsored by the Muslim Brotherhood through at least two individuals. One was Mahmud Abouhalima, a member of the Brotherhood who had worked with the CIA in Afghanistan and networked with radical Muslims and Black Panthers in the United States. The other was Mustafa Shalabi who was the director of Abdullah Azzam's Al Kifah Center in Brooklyn.[157]

After Rahman set up his mosque in New Jersey he and his associates began to pressure Shalabi to turn over control of the Al Kifah Center and its $2 million in assets to Sheikh Rahman. Shalabi backed down in the face of this threat and made plans to leave Brooklyn for Peshawar, Pakistan in March of 1991. The man chosen to succeed Shalabi as director of the Center was a Lebanese-American named Wadih el-Hage, a man

---

[155] *Blowback*, Mary Ann Weaver, 05-1996, *The Atlantic* online
[156] *Ennemies & 'Assets'*, William Norman Grigg, 03-1997, *The New American*
[157] Ibid.

closely-affiliated with the Muslim Brotherhood (most likely a member) who lived at the time in Arlington, Texas. The transition was complicated however, by the murder of Shalabi on February 26, and although el-Hage was in Brooklyn at the time he did not take over the Al Kifah Center after Shalabi's sudden death. Instead he returned to his home in Arlington where he continued his work brokering auto deals to the Middle East. About two years later he was called to Sudan where he worked for Osama bin Laden traveling and selling the agricultural merchandise from bin Laden's businesses. Eventually he became bin Laden's personal secretary. Today he is in a U.S. jail for his involvement with Al Qaeda and connection to the African embassy bombings of 1998, even though he returned to the United States in 1997.[158]

In Brooklyn the Al Kifah Center came under the complete control of Sheikh Rahman's network. In September of 1992 the network brought Ramzi Yousef into the United States. Yousef is now generally recognized as the mastermind of the 1993 World Trade Center bombing, and his case presents an interesting challenge. He entered the United States as Ramzi Yousef on an Iraqi passport. He had no visa, but was given political asylum. Some months later he visited the Pakistani consulate and, after presenting the required documentation, was given a passport under the name Abdul Basit Karim. The U.S. Government's investigation of Ramzi Yousef concluded that Abdul Basit Karim was indeed his true identity.

---

[158] *"Osama bin Laden - the Past,"* Steve Emerson, IASCP.com

Abdul Basit Karim was born in Kuwait in 1968 to a Pakistani father and Palestinian mother. His father was an employee of Kuwait Airlines. In 1984 Karim moved to Britain and began his college education. He took English language courses at the Oxford College of Further Education and attended the West Glamorgen Institute in Swansea, where he graduated with a degree in electronic engineering in 1989. According to Ramzi Yousef's own confession, taken after he was finally arrested and brought to the U.S. in 1995, he was recruited into the Islamist movement in 1987 while living in Swansea after he was approached by local members of the Muslim Brotherhood. In the summer of 1988 he traveled to Pakistan where he attended one of the many Brotherhood-sponsored mujahedin training camps. After graduating with his degree in 1989 he was injured in a bomb blast in Karachi while he was trying to perfect his skills as a bomb-maker. During Iraq's invasion of Kuwait he was in Kuwait collaborating with the Iraqis, as charged by the Kuwaiti Interior Minister, and then prior to Desert Storm he fled to the Philippines where he offered his expertise in bomb-making to the fledgling Islamist groups that were beginning to make their presence known. Abdul Basit Karim, a.k.a. Ramzi Yousef, was a Muslim Brotherhood operative and expert bomb maker, and the network brought him to the United States in late 1992 for the sole purpose of destroying the World Trade Center.[159]

A different theory on Ramzi Yousef's true identity that has unfortunately achieved wide-spread coverage must also be addressed. In the aftermath of the 1993 attack

---

[159] "*The Past As Prologue,*" Russ Baker, 10-2001, salon.com

there was a serious effort on the part of many conservatives to implicate Saddam Hussein's Iraq as the state-sponsor of the 1993 bombing. This theory was spearheaded by well-respected analyst Laurie Mylroie, and subsequently supported by former head of the CIA James Woolsey, who was grasping for anything to mask the CIA's own involvement in the bombing that occurred while he was director. The Iraq theory claims that Abdul Basit Karim was a mild-mannered academic who was **murdered** by Iraqi Intelligence during their occupation of Kuwait in 1990, and that Karim's identity was stolen and given to "Iraqi super-agent" Ramzi Yousef. This theory is almost entirely based on the fact that the Kuwaiti documents of Karim had been obviously tampered with prior to 1993 when they were brought forward during the investigation of the WTC bombing. Mylroie and company concluded that the Iraqis must have been responsible for this and that the tampering had been done to allow Yousef to take over Karim's identity. The fingerprints between Karim and Yousef matched, and so the tampering was alleged by Mylroie to have also included switching fingerprints. This theory was quickly supported by a number of conservatives in the United States, and also by several prominent journalists in Great Britain.[160]

Mylroie does not consider the possibility that the documents may have been tampered with to cover up Karim's collaboration with the Iraqi invaders and his involvement with the Muslim Brotherhood which supported Iraq during the invasion. Mylroie's elaborate

---

[160] *"Who is Ramzi Youssef? And Why It Matters,"* Laurie Mylroie, Winter 95/96, *National Interest*

theory was also understandably supported by several members of the faculty of Karim's Swansea University. Ken Reid, the deputy principle, claimed that Karim's height and weight were different than Yousef's. He also stated that Yousef's deformed eye and smaller ears and mouth did not match Karim's.[161] Brad White, a former Senate investigator and CBS newsman also took up Mylroie's cause and interviewed teachers who had known Karim. *"Two people had a good memory of Abdul Basit but, shown photos of Yousef, were unable to make a positive identification. They both felt that while there was some similarity in looks, it was not the same person. 'Our feeling is that Ramzi Yousef is probably not Basit', White was told."*[162] However, these alleged differences can be partly explained by Yousef's bomb-making accident in Karachi in 1989 that resulted in facial injuries and a lengthy hospitalization.

Another angle was attempted by a British journalist who described Yousef's command of the English language as "appalling" and theorized that he could not be the same Karim who had lived in Britain for four years and attended language courses at Oxford.[163] This theory falls flat when faced with Yousef's performance during his trial: *"He insisted on representing himself at the first trial; he cut a sharp figure in a tailored, double-breasted suit, frequently turned on the charm and generally represented himself surprisingly well, even getting hostile witnesses to contradict*

---

[161] *"Terrorists' trade in stolen identities,"* Daniel McGrory, 9-22-01, *The Times* UK

[162] *"Of Passports and Fingerprints,"* internet article

[163] *"Terrorists' trade in stolen identities,"* Daniel McGrory, 9-22-01, *The Times* UK

themselves."[164] Could his English have been that *"appalling"* for him to represent himself so well at his American trial?

Simon Reeve in his book *The New Jackals* confronts the allegations that Yousef was not Karim. He mentions Neil Herman, the head of the FBI investigation into the 1993 bombing, and he also quotes from several of Basit's friends from his days at Swansea,

"...Neil Herman and the FBI are convinced Yousef and Karim are one and the same, and several former students remember and identify 'Ramzi,' their 'temperamental' and 'volatile' former mate. *'One minute he was your friend, and the next . . .'* said one Welsh student. Another former student from South Wales remembers a mutual friend of his and Yousef's - a Briton from an Asian family - mentioning a political conversation the two men had. *'He's a real nutter,'* the man was told. Another student cut out and kept newspaper articles from Yousef's trial. When Yousef was still on the run he remembers comparing the newspaper pictures with those in his albums. *'That's my friend Jane, she's a teacher,'* he would say to friends looking at the albums, *'that's my friend Phil, he's an engineer, and then* [turning to the articles] *that's my friend Ramzi, the international terrorist and most wanted man in the world.*"[165]

In any case, it is understandable that the faculty of Karim's university would like to distance their institution from Yousef the terrorist mastermind, and it

[164] *"The Past As Prologue,"* Russ Baker, 10-2001, salon.com
[165] *The New Jackals,* Simon Reeve, 1999, p.251

is understandable that conservatives like Mylroie were so willing to look for a "higher power" responsible for the WTC bombing. A higher power did exist, but it was not Iraq, and most conservatives are so completely anglophile in their outlook that they find it impossible to look critically at Britain, which is where the Muslim Brotherhood is based.

The question of Yousef's true identity was finally settled in the few weeks after September 11, 2001. Former CIA chief James Woolsey was dispatched to London to gather whatever proof he could that Iraq was at least partially responsible for the attacks. His trip was independently sponsored by Paul Wolfowitz, the hawkish deputy defense secretary, creating a rift within the Bush Administration and angering the state department and the CIA.[166] Woolsey focused on the allegations that lead hijacker Mohammed Atta had met with Iraqi Intelligence in Prague, and he also looked into Yousef's alleged Iraqi connection: *"Another bit of intrigue that Woolsey has been exploring while in Britain involves a convicted Kuwaiti terrorist known as Ramzi Youssef, whose real name is Abdul Basit. Woolsey claims that Youssef is an Iraqi agent who kidnapped Basit and stole his identity. Woolsey's sleuthing has made him something of a laughingstock among British police and intelligence, who are "bemused" by his activities, according to one British official. But Woolsey's own lack of credibility hasn't stopped the mainstream media from quoting him extensively to whip up anti-Iraq hysteria."* [167]

---

[166] *"Hawks try to implicate Iraq by hunting for evidence in UK,"* 10-2001, DAWN.com
[167] Ibid.

Woolsey met with British Intelligence who, to Woolsey's dismay, agreed with the long-standing conclusion of the American investigators in Yousef's trial and confirmed that Ramzi Yousef *really was* Abdul Basit Karim, and not an Iraqi impostor. The matter has since been dropped, although Laurie Mylroie continues to believe that the British are going out of their way to cover for Saddam,[168] even while Tony Blair scrambles for reasons to support Bush's plans to invade Iraq.

Abdul Basit Karim, a.k.a. Ramzi Yousef, fled the United States immediately after the February 26, 1993 bombing to Karachi, Pakistan. In 1994 he appeared back in the Philippines where he joined up with the Muslim Brotherhood cell that had been established to support the new **Abu Sayyaf** terrorist group in Mindanao. Karim met up with Mohammed Jamal Khalifa, a brother-in- law of Osama bin Laden, who had helped to finance the initial creation of the Abu Sayyaf group that is named after militant Islamist Dr. Abdurrab Rasul Sayyaf.[169] Dr. Sayyaf received his doctorate from Cairo's Al Azhar University and became one of the most important theologians in Afghanistan. He founded the University of Sawal al-Jihad in Peshawar around 1990 and is today an outspoken militant critic of the new Karzai government in Afghanistan and an enemy of the United States. Abu Sayyaf is seen by many as an Al Qaeda front group, but in reality it is a Muslim Brotherhood group that was planned long before Osama bin Laden emerged as the "international terrorist mastermind."

---

[168] PBS Frontline, interview with Laurie Mylroie
[169] "*The Terror Lurking Within Asia*," John Moy, 10-11-02, SCMP.com

In the Philippines Abdul Basit Karim, a.k.a. Yousef, also interacted closely with his uncle Khalid Shaikh Mohammed, who is now understood to be the operational mastermind of the attacks of September 11, and suspected as the mastermind of WTC 1993. Like Karim, Mohammed was born in Kuwait, but moved to Pakistan.[170] Kuwaiti records show that Karim's entire family moved from Kuwait to Pakistan on August 26, 1990 during the Iraqi occupation.[171] Indian Intelligence believes that the entire family is originally from the Balochistan province of Pakistan and that Karim was only raised in Kuwait.[172] In any case, Karim and his uncle Khalid, who once attended a North Carolina college,[173] are the terrorists who originally conceived of the operation that was finally pulled off on September 11. Philippine Police uncovered the plot, known as Operation Bojinka, after raiding Karim's apartment due to an alarm raised from a bomb-making accident. A computer was recovered which contained plans to place bombs on eleven U.S. jetliners timed to go off simultaneously. One of the captured members of the cell, Abdul Hakim Murad, later admitted under interrogation that phase two of the plan was to hijack jetliners and fly them into targets such as the CIA headquarters, the White House, the Pentagon and possibly some skyscrapers. Murad was sure of this because he had attended several American flight schools, in Texas, New York and North Carolina, and

[170] *"Terrorist Plot Years in the Making,"* Daniel Rubin and Michael Dorgan, Knight Ridder Newspapers
[171] *"Of Passports and Fingerprints,"* internet article
[172] *"Antecedents of Ramzi Ahmed Youssef,"* 10-1996 , SAPRA INDIA
[173] *"The Left's Acrobatic Logic on Terror,"* David Harsanyi, 6-11-02, Capitalism Magazine.com

he was to be one of the suicide pilots.[174]

Uncovering the plot and disrupting the terrorist cell was a triumph for Philippine Intelligence, and the CIA awarded Senior Inspector Aida D. Fariscal a certificate of merit *"In recognition of your personal outstanding efforts and co-operation."*[175] The CIA then promptly forgot all about Operation Bojinka.

Karim, a.k.a. Ramzi Yousef, was able to barely escape from the Philippines and avoid arrest, but he did leave behind several technical reference books that he had stolen from the Swansea library (further confirming his identity as Karim).[176] He made his way back to Pakistan where he easily went underground in the extensive Islamist network. He would have continued to have been a key figure in the global terror network, but he was betrayed by one of his closest associates. A South African Muslim recruited by Karim offered information on Karim's whereabouts in return for the $2 million reward offered by the American government for his arrest. Karim was apprehended in his apartment by U.S. and Pakistani security officials on February 7, 1995. The informant collected the $2 million reward and now lives in the United States under a new identity with his family, sheltered by the Witness Protection Program.[177] Karim was subsequently deported to the United States and tried and convicted for the WTC bombing. "Ramzi Yousef" now serves a life sentence of 240 years.

[174] *"Dropping the Ball,"* Reed Irvine, World Net Daily .com
[175] *"Operation Bojinka's Bombshell,"* Matthew Brzezinski (Zbigniew's nephew), 1-2-02, *The Toronto Star*
[176] 19b. Reeve, p. 89
[177] *"The Past As Prologue,"* Russ Baker, 10-2001, salon.com

Karim's uncle escaped out of the Philippines as well. However, in 1996 while he was in the Persian Gulf kingdom of Qatar a deal was struck between the Qatar government and the FBI to detain Khalid Sheikh Mohammed and turn him over to the United States. The FBI dispatched a team to Qatar who waited for their prize in a hotel, but at the last minute the deal fell through. Apparently a "higher power" had intervened at the last moment and Mohammed was spirited away. Khalid Sheikh Mohammed escaped to Prague, of all places, where he set up a new headquarters under the name Mustaf Nasir. Who could have possibly intervened to disrupt an important deal that was at the final stage between two sovereign governments? The person who intervened in the deal was reportedly the government minister in charge of religious affairs.[178] The other factor that must be considered is that Qatar is the home of one of the most prominent and outspoken Muslim Brotherhood theologians, Dr. Yusuf al-Qaradawi, the Dean of Islamic Studies at the University of Qatar, who also works out of London as head of the Islamic Council of Europe.[179] Khalid Sheikh Mohammed's stay in Qatar had to have been hosted by the Muslim Brotherhood, and only the Muslim Brotherhood possessed the influence and power necessary to disrupt the deal to deport Mohammed to American authorities.

Khalid Sheikh Mohammed is the key to uncovering the entire conspiracy surrounding September 11, yet

---

[178] *Breakdown: How America's Intelligence Failures Led to September 11*, Bill Gertz, 2002, pp. 55-56
[179] Qaradawi: London, Qatar

investigative journalists around the world are unable to uncover hardly anything about the man's life. *Wall Street Journal* reporter Daniel Pearl was kidnapped and brutally murdered for pursuing his investigation of Khalid Sheikh Mohammed into Pakistan, and the dramatically edited high-tech video of his execution by beheading was disseminated worldwide via the internet as a **warning**. When the US Congress began its inquiry into the events of September 11 they found that **CIA chief George Tenet** prevented the declassification of all information regarding Khalid Shaikh Mohammed, and Mohammed's name was not even allowed to be mentioned in the inquiry's report. Tenet knows that a critical examination of Khalid Sheikh Mohammed will reveal Mohammed's close ties to the Muslim Brotherhood, and subsequently the Muslim Brotherhood's ties to the elite intelligence organizations of the West. Mohammed was a CIA asset, as was "Ramzi Yousef." They were a part of the Muslim Brotherhood organization but they were Muslims in name only. The Philippine investigation revealed that Mohammed and his nephew "Yousef" both enjoyed drinking, partying, visiting strip bars and pursuing the local women.[180] It was the same thing with many of the hijackers of 9-11 as they passed the time in Florida up to their operation. This stands in stark contrast to Osama bin Laden, who would put his fingers to his ears when music played while out in public in Sudan.[181] Osama bin Laden was loosely connected to the events of September 11, but only because the international Islamist movement is so small, and he played little if

---

[180] *Non-Muslim lifestyle: Khalid Sheikh Mohammed*, Ramzi Youssef
[181] Biography of bin Laden in Sudan

any part in planning and executing the operation. The truth may only be found through Khalid Sheikh Mohammed, and too many powerful interests are determined to hide that truth.

VII. Bin Laden's Money Problems

By the end of 1993, after serving al-Turabi and the Muslim Brotherhood dutifully for two years, bin Laden began to feel a cash crunch. He was not allowed to withdraw funds at will from the 'Brotherhood Group' financial network that he had helped set up after the fall of the BCCI because it was not his network. He was dependent on his masters do disperse these funds to him and at this time the Brotherhood did not see any cause for which bin Laden needed funding.

The primary reason for bin Laden going broke was that the Saudi government had blocked all of his assets and bank accounts. This fact is related by a number of sources, including Robinson, and the unnamed author (I have reasons to believe he is Dr. Saad al-Fagih) of a biography of bin Laden posted at PBS.

To remedy this situation Osama bin Laden did what many other Saudi dissidents have done over the past several decades: he moved to London and established an organization to publicize his group and to accept donations from the millions of affluent Muslims living in Britain. This was done by the aforementioned Dr. Saad al-Fagih, who fled Saudi Arabia and set up his **Movement for Islamic Reform in Arabia**, and also by Dr. Muhammed al-Massari who fled Saudi Arabia and set up the **Committee for the Defense of Legitimate Rights** (CDLR).

The fact that Bin Laden lived in London for a short period of time received a great deal of publicity in 1999 with the publication of Yossef Bodansky's book, *Bin*

Laden - the Man Who Declared War on America. Bodansky's claim was challenged by several London journalists, and most notably by CNN's resident terrorist "expert" Peter Bergen, the author of *Holy War, Inc.*, who ridiculed the possibility. However, bin Laden's time in London has since been confirmed by Saudi-based journalist Adam Robinson in his book *Bin Laden - Behind the Mask of the Terrorist.* His biography, published late in 2001, draws from interviews with Osama's immediate family and gives a detailed account of bin Laden's three months in England at the beginning of 1994.

Upon arriving Bin Laden bought a house *"on, or near, Harrow Road in the Wembley area of London. He paid cash, and used an intermediary as the named owner."*[182] Bin Laden's most important task was setting up his organization, the **Advice and Reformation Committee**, to disperse his press releases and to receive donations. After bin Laden left a fellow Saudi dissident, Khaled al-Fawwaz ran the ARC from London, keeping in touch with bin Laden via satellite phone, and distributing his statements to the many Arab-language newspapers based in London. As mentioned in Part One, bin Laden also established relations with two London residents that were crucial to crafting his image as an international spokesman for, and mastermind of, the militant Islamist movement over the years. The first was Abdel Bari Atwan, the editor of the Arabic newspaper *Al-Quds Al-Arabi*, and the other was radical cleric, and Muslim Brother, Sheikh Omar Bakri Muhammad, who called himself *"the voice of Osama bin Laden"* and directed the extremist **Islamic**

---

[182] *Bin Laden: Behind the Mask of the Terrorist*, Adam Robinson, 2001, p. 168

Liberation Party and the *al-Muhajiroun* organization out of his London mosque.

Robinson also relates that bin Laden found the time to do some sightseeing. He writes, *"Osama was given to sending postcards. This paper trail shows that he toured the Tower of London and the Imperial War Museum. He also left the south of England on at least one occasion and was one of the million people every year who visit Edinburgh Castle in the Scottish capital."*[183]

Robinson also describes bin Laden's reaction upon attending two important Arsenal football games, including a March 15 match that saw Arsenal defeat Torino and advance into the semifinals of a European tournament. Bin Laden commented on the excitement and passion of the fans, and later told his friends and family that it was like nothing he had ever seen. When he returned to Sudan he brought back with him Arsenal Club memorabilia, including a jersey for his fifteen-year-old son Abdullah.[184]

Bin Laden's London excursion was cut short by interference from Saudi Arabia. Bin Laden was not a terrorist "mastermind," but he was a high-level militant operative of the Muslim Brotherhood, and he was the most highly-connected Saudi to ever publicly turn against his government. According to Robinson further pressure was placed on the Saudi regime by Yemen, and also in early 1994 by President Mubarak of Egypt.[185]

---

[183] Robinson, p. 169
[184] Robinson, p. 169
[185] Robinson, p. 172

Both governments were receiving intelligence that Sudan was aiding terrorists trying to destabilize their regimes. Robinson describes Saudi Arabia's response to the bin Laden problem,

"In April 1994, his Saudi citizenship was revoked for *'irresponsible behaviour,'* and he was informed that he was no longer welcome in his land of birth because he had *'committed acts that adversely affected the brotherly relations of the kingdom of Saudi Arabia and other countries.'"[186]

In England the Saudi government demanded that Britain turn him over to be extradited. Instead he was allowed to quietly leave the UK and return to Sudan. Bin Laden's first move after coming home was to issue a statement denouncing the Saudi decision revoking his citizenship. His response was that he was not dependent upon his Saudi Arabian nationality to define himself as a Muslim. Several weeks later his ARC sprang to life in London, describing itself in press releases as *"a political group that aimed to be an effective opposition inside and outside of the one-party system in Saudi Arabia."*[187] Robinson p. 173

For the next several years in Sudan bin Laden continued to be wary of his finances. His own enterprises commanded a very high overhead and so he needed a continual cash flow. In a 1996 interview with Abdel Bari Atwan's *Al-Quds Al-Arabi* he claimed that he had lost over *"$150 million on farming and construction*

---

[186] Robinson, p. 172
[187] Robinson, p. 173

projects" during his time in Sudan.[188] He never ran out of money but he began to be more careful of his spending. The 'Brotherhood Group' may have been a financial network that never lacked for funds, but bin Laden's personal accounts were not endless. This fact became clear through the testimony of several Al Qaeda operatives who were arrested in the aftermath of the African embassy bombings of 1998, and from the testimony of Al Qaeda defectors.

One defector, Jamal al-Fadl, who at one time ran bin Laden's payroll, complained of his $500 a month salary and compared it with the $1200 salary some of the Egyptian employees were making. Bin Laden explained that they were paid more because they could command higher salaries back in Egypt and he wanted to keep them in the group. Al-Fadl later defected after stealing $110,000 from bin Laden.[189]

Another defector, L'Houssaine Kerchtou, became upset with bin Laden after he refused to pay for an emergency caesarian operation needed for his preganant wife. He testified that, *"Since the end of '94 - '95 we have a crisis in Al Qaeda. Osama bin Laden himself, he was talking to us and saying that there is no money and he lost all his money, and he shouldn't extend a lot of things and he reduced the salary of people."* Kerchtou also testified that bin Laden refused to pay to have his pilot's license renewed. One would think that licensed pilots would be considered a tremendous asset for the infamous Al Qaeda terrorist

---

188 *"Tracing Bin Laden's Money,"* ICT
189 *"Trial Poked Holes,"* New York Times, *"Cross Examination..."*

organization.[190]

In late 2001 *Al-Quds Al-Arabi* published a series of reports on Bin Laden's life in Sudan. The reports characterized his stay as "negative," and described the terrible financial cost to him, *"The Sudan era was important despite its negative impact on Bin Ladin. The Sudanese viewed him as an investor who came to support the Islamic project declared by Dr. Hasan al-Turabi, the spiritual leader of the Sudanese Islamic revolution... On one side, it was a bitter experience for Bin Ladin that* **cost him huge amounts of money** *but on the other side, it was a time when many of the subsequent ideas and acts were fermented."*[191]

Other problems arose within Al Qaeda while bin Laden was based in Sudan. When Sheikh Rahman was taken into American custody following the 1993 WTC bombing a number of bin Laden's Egyptian employees demanded that plans be made to strike back at America, but bin Laden refused. Because of this a number of them left Al Qaeda in disgust. Later on, due to Libyan pressure on Sudan, bin Laden attempted to send his Libyan operatives home. He explained the situation to them and offered plane tickets for themselves and their families, but they were so disgusted to see bin Laden cave in to the political pressure that they refused the offer and walked out.[192]

The embassy bombings trial did a great deal to undermine the notion that Osama bin Laden and his Al

---

[190] *"Trial Reveals a Conspiracy..."* CNN.com,

[191] *"Bin Ladin's Life in Sudan,"* Al Quds Al Arabi

[192] *"Trial Poked Holes,"* New York Times

The Globalists & the Islamists

Qaeda organization was a tremendously wealthy, invincible, seamless, secretive terror machine capable of striking anywhere in the world. Up until the middle of 2001 the New York Times was publishing articles such as the one on May 31 by Benjamin Weiser entitled *"Trial Poked Holes in Image of bin Laden's Terrorist Group,"* but these reports were not enough to shatter the illusion, and September 11 brought it back with a vengeance.

Bin Laden's money woes and other internal problems may be one explanation for the apparent betrayal of bin Laden by Hassan al-Turabi and the Sudanese government. According to American businessman Mansoor Ijaz, who met with Turabi in July of 1996, Sudan made several offers to hand bin Laden over to the United States in return for the lifting of economic sanctions.[193] The first offer were was made in February of 1996, but it was ignored by the Clinton Administration, even though a State Department report, **Patterns of Global Terrorism** was calling bin Laden *"one of the most significant financial sponsors of Islamic extremist activities in the world today."*

The offer was repeated in May of 1996 as bin Laden was preparing to move his organization to Afghanistan, but likewise ignored. Even after bin Laden left Sudan the government made offers to supply the Clinton Administration with information. According to a Newsday.com article Ijaz relayed these offers, but the White House remained uninterested,

---

[193] *"Missed Chance,"* Newsday.com

"On a subsequent visit to Sudan, he said, he met with the Sudanese intelligence chief, Gutbi al-Mahdi. *'If you can persuade your government to come here, this is what can be made available to them,'* **said al-Mahdi, as reported by Ijaz, gesturing at three stacks of files before him.** *'We have the entire network, not just bin Laden or Hezbollah. We understand everything going on in the Islamic world.'"*[194]

According to a January 6, 2002 article in The Sunday Times of London, in a post-9/11 dinner party in Manhattan, Clinton admitted that letting Osama bin Laden go was probably *"the biggest mistake of my presidency."*

But the question arises, was the offer genuine? Was Sudan willing to betray "the entire network" of militant Islam? Ijaz had met with National Security Council deputy Sandy Berger and Susan Rice, the senior advisor on African affairs to relay the offers. Rice subsequently explained that the offers were ignored because of Sudan's proven track record of duplicity,

"The Sudanese are one of the most slippery, dishonest governments in the world. The only thing that matters is what they do, not what they say they're going to do. They're very good at saying one thing and doing another."[195]

Perhaps Sudan was willing to turn over bin Laden, but

---

[194] *"Missed Chance,"* Newsday.com
[195] *"Missed Chance,"* Newsday.com

turning over bin Laden would have been but a small blow to the Islamist Movement. The International Muslim Brotherhood would have retained control over the financial network set up in part by bin Laden and it would have continued its war against the Middle East's moderate regimes, and against the West, without hardly missing a beat. Osama bin Laden was expendable.

Peter Goodgame

VIII. The Brotherhood Revolution Continues

After bin Laden returned from his visit to England in 1994 things began to heat up in the Muslim world. After publicly revoking bin Laden's citizenship the Saudi regime faced increasing fundamentalist unrest at home. The House of Saud was walking a fine line - it supported jihad and the expansion of Islam around the world, and capitalized on its role as guardians of the holy places, but at the same time the family's decadence, corruption and personal immoralities were becoming more and more evident at home. It was only a matter of time before this hypocrisy became a problem and the jihad turned back on its maker.

One of the loudest dissident voices within Saudi Arabia was a militant sheik named Salman bin Fahd al-Udah. He was well known to bin Laden and to the thousands of Saudi "Afghans" who lived restlessly in the kingdom after returning from the battlefield. The Saudi regime began to view Sheikh Udah with greater and greater worry, and in September of 1994 they arrested him. Only a few days later an organization of anonymous origin called the **Battalions of Faith** made the headlines when it issued an ultimatum to the Saudi government that demanded the release of Sheikh Udah within five days, or else face a campaign of terrorism against the Saudi and American governments.

The Saudi government ignored the warnings and nothing came of the threat, but Bodansky writes that it was notable because it was the *"first initiative taken by the Saudi Islamist system... the first threat of violence against the*

House of al-Saud." This ultimatum was the first *"overt communiqué of an Islamist terrorist organization inside Saudi Arabia."*[196]

In April of 1995 the Saudi Islamists received a boost in the form of a recorded message given by Sheikh Udah that had been smuggled out and distributed to his supporters. Bodansky describes how important this message was:

"The lecture, titled 'Death Workmanship,' covered the whole logic of the relationship between Islamist and Western civilization and amounted to a declaration of an armed jihad against the House of al-Saud. It provided justification for perpetual confrontation...
'Death Workmanship' amounted to a fatwa, that is, a religious decree, ordering the launch of jihad against the Saudi royal family. Sheikh Udah decreed that any rejection of jihad in favor of another form of resistance was apostasy, a capital offence according to Muslim law, which left the believer with no alternative but to fight..."[197]
Bodansky pp.117-118

This message from Sheikh Udah fired up the resistance to the Saudi regime at home and around the world. According to Bodansky the London-based CDLR (mentioned above) is *"the largest and best-organized Saudi Islamic opposition group,"* and with the issuance of Sheikh

---

196 *Bin Laden: The Man Who Declared War on America,* Yossef Bodansky, 1999, p. 117
197 Ibid. pp. 117-118

Udah's message the organization changed from being moderate and diplomatic to becoming a supporter of armed resistance to the Saudi regime, a change reflected in their own statements and press releases.

The Saudi Islamist network struck for real on November 13, 1995, when a car bomb exploded in Riyadh destroying an American-leased building and killing six people including five Americans. Robinson writes that the bomb was made out of 200 lbs. of Semtex military-grade explosives, and that it shattered windows in a one-mile radius. Immediately a number of underground Islamists groups claimed responsibility for the attack.

Bodansky writes that the Armed Islamic Movement, the Muslim Brotherhood's loose-knit unofficial jihad organization, claimed credit *"by disseminating through AIM-affiliated venues a communiqué in the name of a previously unknown group calling itself The Militant Partisans of God Organization. The AIM communiqué also stressed that the Riyadh operation was 'the first of our jihad operations.'"*[198]

The Muslim Brotherhood was taking advantage of the Saudi political climate and had joined in the movement to topple the House of Saud. This was only a secondary operation, however. The primary goal for the Muslim Brotherhood in 1995 was to destroy its historical enemy, the secular government of Egypt.

In March of 1995 Hassan al-Turabi convened a meeting in Khartoum with three of the leading Egyptian

---

[198] Ibid. p. 141

Islamists: Dr. Ayman al-Zawahiri, the head of Egyptian **Islamic Jihad**, along with Mustafa Hamza and Rifai Ahmed Taha, both of **al-Jamaah al-Islamiyah** (the Islamic Group). Zawahiri was based in Geneva where his organization was directed from a Muslim Brotherhood mosque (p.125). Mustafa Hamza was based in London and Khartoum, while Rifai Ahmed Taha was based in London and Peshawar, Pakistan. It was at this meeting that the plan to assassinate President Hosni Mubarak of Egypt was agreed upon. The attack would be made during Mubarak's scheduled diplomatic visit to Addis Ababa, Ethiopia in late June.[199] p. 123

Weeks later the plan was presented at a larger Islamist meeting in Khartoum. It was thought that Mubarak's assassination would create the diversion for an Islamist coup in Egypt, followed quickly by the fall of the House of Saud and the overthrow of the Persian Gulf states. Mustafa Hamza was chosen to coordinate the uprising within Egypt and Ayman al-Zawahiri was picked as the operational director of the actual attack on Mubarak.[200]

In late May Turabi traveled to Paris for "medical treatment," from where he made a quick secret visit to Geneva to meet again with Zawahiri. Two weeks later Zawahiri made an "inspection visit" to Khartoum, and he was also able to travel to Ethiopia using a forged passport to go over the plan on the ground. He then returned to Geneva where the final meeting of the top-

[199] Ibid. pp. 123, 125
[200] Ibid. p. 124

level operational leaders took place in safety on June 23.[201]

The plan was to use three teams to attack Mubarak's convoy of vehicles as it left the airport and traveled to the convention center half a mile away. The first team would attack the convoy with machine guns from a number of rooftop locations near the airport. This was supposed to slow the convoy allowing the second team, armed with RPGs, to come in and blast the president's car and/or any other official Egyptian vehicles in range. If Mubarak's vehicle managed to escape it would face the third team, which was simply a single massively-armed car bomb driven by a suicide bomber. Zawahiri's intelligence contacts had related that Mubarak's driver was instructed to travel full speed ahead to their destination if anything happened, and the car bomb was the last chance to take him out.

The plan failed for a number of reasons. First, Mubarak's entourage was delayed in coordinating the convoy, and because Ethiopian police had extra time to secure the route the RPG squad was told to repackage their rockets for security reasons. Then without notice Mubarak announced that whoever was ready should join his convoy to journey to the convention center. He was not willing to wait around for the entire convoy to assemble, and for this reason the hit teams had no advance notice and were caught with their RPGs packaged away. The final decision that saved Mubarak's life was the choice made once the small arms fire erupted and the convoy jammed together and stopped.

---

[201] Ibid. p. 125

The driver simply turned the car around and sped back to the safety of the airport. The car bomber never even had the chance to get near Mubarak's limousine, which happened to be his special Mercedes brought from Egypt that was bulletproof as well as RPG- proof.[202]

Bodansky describes the ramifications of this failed plot, **"The attempt on President Hosni Mubarak's life in Addis Ababa, Ethiopia, on June 26, 1995, was a milestone in the evolution of the Islamist struggle for control over the Arab world and the Hub of Islam. Operations of such magnitude, even if ultimately claimed by or attributed to obscure terrorist organizations, are actually instruments of state policy and are carried out on behalf of the highest echelons of the terrorism-sponsoring states. The assassination attempt, a strategic gambit sponsored by Sudan and Iran, had regional and long- term effects. Although President Mubarak survived and the Islamist popular uprising envisaged by the conspirators failed to materialize in Egypt, the mere attempt gave a major boost to the Islamist surge throughout the region."[203]** p. 121

On July 4 responsibility for the attack was claimed by the **Islamic Group** (al-Jamaah al- Islamiyah), the terrorist organization of the imprisoned Sheikh Omar Abdul Rahman. It was claimed that the attack was made in honor of an Islamist commander killed by Egyptian police in 1994.

[202] Ibid. pp. 130-131
[203] Ibid. p. 121

Egypt was quick to blame Sudan for sponsoring the attack, and Ethiopia and the United States, followed by the UN, blamed Sudan as well. The evidence was overwhelming that Sudan had housed, trained and financed the terrorists, and Sudan's guilt was confirmed by their refusal to turn over three of the terrorists accused of conducting the operation. Because of this the UN imposed diplomatic sanctions, and the United States evacuated its Khartoum embassy, expelled a Sudanese diplomat and imposed diplomatic and economic sanctions. Sudan's time as an effective haven for the militant Islamic movement was up. Turabi had to quickly change his policies to avoid any serious actions against Sudan and to preserve his Islamist regime. One of his conciliatory gestures, however empty, was to offer Osama bin Laden over to the United States. The Clinton Administration didn't buy it.

The next assault on the government of Egypt occurred on November 19, 1995, just six days after the Riyadh bombing of American servicemen. A small car rammed its way through the gate of the Egyptian embassy in Islamabad, Pakistan and seconds later a small explosion occurred in an area where visitors were standing in line for visas. The explosion, reportedly a suicide bomber who had jumped out of the car, created a diversion and in the commotion a van loaded with 900 lbs. of explosives rammed into the front of the embassy. This huge explosion created a crater twenty feet wide and ten feet deep. Nineteen people were killed and scores more were wounded.

Soon afterward three main Egyptian terror groups claimed responsibility. The **Islamic Group** of Sheikh

Rahman, led by Mustafa Hamza and Rifai Ahmed Taha, claimed that the bombing was done in opposition to President Mubarak. The Islamic Group later withdrew its claim of responsibility. The next claim was from Ayman al-Zawahiri's **Islamic Jihad**, which stated the names of the attackers, the "martyrs" who perpetrated the attack. The last claim came from the Zawahiri-affiliated **International Justice Group**, and the attack was said to have been made by *"the squad of the martyr Khalid Islambouli,"* referring to the executed assassin of President Anwar Sadat of Egypt.[204]

Bodansky offers his conclusion as to who was responsible for this attack on the Egyptian government, **"Like the assassination attempt on President Mubarak, the Islamabad bombing operation was conducted under the tight control of and financed by the higher Islamist headquarters in Western Europe - Ayman al- Zawahiri in Geneva and his new second-in-command, Yassir Tawfiq Sirri in London."[205] p. 144**

By the end of 1995 Sudan was feeling the full effects of its sponsorship of the militant Islamist movement. The economy was in terrible shape and sanctions were prohibiting any sort of substantive economic investment or aid from the outside, and Egypt and Saudi Arabia were on the verge of taking direct military action. Because of these pressures General Bashir began to lessen his support for Hassan Turabi's Islamist experiment and leaned on him to cool things down for a while. Sudan's time as a Muslim Brotherhood base was near its end. This was foreseen by the MB and even as the Mubarak assassination plot was being planned their assets were being relocated to the camps of Gulbuddin Hekmatyar in Afghanistan. A year later Osama bin Laden followed suit. He touched down in Jalalabad, Afghanistan on May 18, 1996.

For further information read the following important articles by the CRG's Chaim Kupferberg:

The Mystery Surrounding the Death of John O'Neill:
The Propaganda Preparation for 9/11

Daniel Pearl and the Paymaster of 9/11:
9/11 and The Smoking Gun that Turned On its Tracker

Bibliography

A Century of War - Anglo-American Oil Politics and the New World Order, F. William Engdahl, 1993

A Brutal Friendship - The West and the Arab Elite, Said K. Aburish, 1997

History of Egypt: British Occupation (1882-1952), Arab.net Timeline of Egypt, utexas.edu

The Egypt of Naguib Mahfouz, chronology

MI6 - Inside the Covert World of Her Majesty's Secret Intelligence Service, Stephen Dorril, 2000

The Biography of Dr. Mohammad Mossadegh, jebhemelli.org

Killing Hope - U.S. Military and CIA Interventions Since World War II, William Blum, 1995

MI6 - Inside the Covert World of Her Majesty's Secret Intelligence Service, Stephen Dorril, 2000

Descent to Suez - Foreign Office Diaries 1951-1956, Sir Evelyn Shuckburgh, 1986

Conspirators' Hierarchy: The Committee of 300, Dr. John Coleman, 1992

What Really Happened In Iran, Dr. John Coleman, 1984, special report, World In Review publications

The real Iranian hostage story from the files of Fara Monsoor,
Harry V. Martin, 1995

*The Outlaw Bank: A Wild Ride Into the Secret Heart of
BCCI,* Jonathan Beaty and S.C. Gwynne, 1993

The Nefarious Activities of Pak I.S.I., website

Breaking the Bank, commentary, Wall Street Journal
Europe, 8-03-01

British India, ucla.edu

Killing Hope, William Blum, 1995

Afghanistan- The Bear Trap, the Defeat of a Superpower,
Mohammad Yousaf and Major Mark Adkin, 1992

Bin Laden - The Man Who Declared War On America,
Yossef Bodansky, 1999

Holy War, Wilhelm Dietl, 1983

Hostage To Khomeini, Robert Dreyfuss, 1980

What the Malthusians Say, from *The American Almanac,*
1994

Where On Earth Are We Going? Maurice Strong, 2000

Bin Laden: Behind the Mask of the Terrorist, Adam
Robinson, 2001

In the Name of Osama Bin Laden, Roland Jacquard, 2001

Islam in Central Asia: Afghanistan and Pakistan, Ahmed Rashid, (online PDF article)

Forbidden Truth, Jean-Charles Brisard and Guillaume Dasquie, 2002

Peter Goodgame, Fall 2002
www.redmoonrising.com

www.ingramcontent.com/pod-product-compliance
Lightning Source LLC
Chambersburg PA
CBHW072241270326
41930CB00010B/2220